Gifts From
A Course
in Miracles

Gifts From A Course in Miracles

ACCEPT THIS GIFT
A GIFT OF PEACE
A GIFT OF HEALING

EDITED BY
Frances Vaughan, Ph.D.,
and Roger Walsh, M.D., Ph.D.

Photographs by Jane English, Ph.D.

A JEREMY P. TARCHER / PUTNAM BOOK
published by G. P. Putnam's Sons
New York

A Jeremy P. Tarcher/Putnam Book
Published by G. P. Putnam's Sons
Publishers Since 1838
200 Madison Avenue
New York, NY 10016

Library of Congress Cataloging-in-Publication Data

Course in miracles. Selections.
    Gifts from a Course in miracles/ edited by Frances
Vaughan, Roger Walsh ; photographs by Jane English.
        p.   cm.
    "A Jeremy P. Tarcher/Putnam book."
    Contents: Accept this gift—A gift of peace—A gift of
healing.
    ISBN 0-87477-803-4
    1. Spiritual life.   I. Vaughan, Frances E.   II. Walsh, Roger N.
III. Title.
    [BP605.C6725   1995]   94-47459 CIP
299'.93—dc20

Design by Tanya Maiboroda
Cover design by Susan Shankin
Cover photo © by Art Montes de Oca/FPG International

Printed in the United States of America
6   7   8   9   10

This book is dedicated to universal peace.

Contents

Foreword

The world we live in is neither stable nor kind, and the search for peace is a search for internal sustenance. As it is written in *A Course in Miracles*, peace of mind "is clearly an internal matter." Anyone who has ever sought for peace has found the search itself, at times, as lonely and painful as the life before we embarked upon it.

That's the bad news. The good news is, there's help everywhere, and particularly in books. Throughout the ages, words have been written which lead us up and out of worldly despair. These words are found on stone and clay tablets, on parchment and cave walls, in every language, in hieroglyphs, in tombs and temples, on paper, in books, in computers and in graffiti. Truth has always sought its expression in words.

Just as there are stars and then superstars, there are books and then Great Books. Within the Great Book category, there are THE BOOKS, the great spiritual source materials which contain the words that reveal the highest truths. They are the Bible, the Koran, the Talmud, the I Ching, and others. For many of us, *A Course in Miracles* is one of these. It opens the heart to healing and hope, enlightenment and love.

That is why I first read *A Course in Miracles*, and why I still read it. Great books don't just inform us; they change us. They address not only what we think, but how we think. They spark explosions within our brains and miracles within our hearts.

For me, and for thousands, perhaps millions of other people, *A Course in Miracles* is a miracle in itself—paragraph after paragraph of words that change our minds. Where we had viewed the world through the eyes of fear, suddenly we see new hope. Reading the *Course*, we are startled by its simplicity and awed by the scope of its promise. Whether glancing at a Workbook exercise for a mere moment before running off to work in the morning, or spending hours in retreat and meditation on the huge and myriad themes of faith and forgiveness which the *Course* teaches, we are in the process, through exposure to these ideas on whatever level, of transforming our lives from fear to love.

We do not graduate from *A Course in Miracles*. We merely become more and more consistent in our ability to open our hearts instead of closing them. Books like *Gifts From A Course in Miracles* help us do this, through the constant and gentle reminders of the beautiful gems that fill its pages.

How lucky we are, to be alive on earth at a time when so much wisdom is accumulated, printed, and distributed to whoever wants it. *A Course in Miracles* is one form of universal spiritual wisdom, a curriculum of love and forgiveness. It is not a religion, and not a doctrine. It is an invitation to inner peace.

Gifts From A Course in Miracles is what I call a quiet book, a serious friend. I read books like this in the middle of the night, or on hilltops, or at the beach. I carry it around with me, as a reminder and a teacher. It is a privilege to add my personal bravo to its continued presence in our lives. I know what this book has given to me; I smile at the thought of what it can give to you.

—Marianne Williamson
Los Angeles

Introduction

In the search for peace and healing we are drawn to teachings that combine deep wisdom with great beauty. When we are fortunate enough to find such a teaching, we may also find limits to our capacity to appreciate it, particularly when profound ideas follow one another as rapidly as they do in *A Course in Miracles*. In studying the *Course*, we have therefore found it helpful to separate out specific passages in order to ponder them more fully. This book is a collection of some of our favorites.

Although written in Christian language and style, *A Course in Miracles* clearly embodies the perennial wisdom found at the core of the world's great religions. Because of this universal nature, its significance and appeal transcend traditional boundaries and extend to all who seek answers to the deepest questions of human existence. Some Buddhists feel that the *Course* echoes the words of the Buddha; yogis have remarked that it expresses the wisdom of Vedanta; and psychologists have found that it offers insights comparable to some of the best contemporary thinking about phenomena such as perception, belief, and identity.

The Writing of the *Course*

The *Course* was written through a process of inner dictation by a very reluctant academic psychologist, Helen Schuman. Born to a nonpracticing Jewish family, she had an intense childhood yearning for religious understanding, but had long ago despaired of finding it.

She was assisted during the writing by her colleague William Thetford. Both were successful professors of medical psychology at Columbia University in New York. Neither had any intention of writing anything religious. Indeed, their lives and work were hardly models of spiritual well-being. They were caught up in the harried and often vicious competition and infighting that can occur in prestigious academic centers. Their relationships were certainly in need of healing, and they lived with significant personal and interpersonal strife. Yet, as the *Course* says, "Tolerance for pain may be high, but it is not without limit. Eventually everyone realizes, however dimly, that there must be a better way."

That realization came to Bill Thetford one day when he suddenly announced to Helen, "There must be a better way of living, and I'm determined to find it."

A few weeks later, Helen started having a series of intense visual images. So vivid were these images that initially Helen feared she might be losing her sanity. However, with Bill's encouragement, she allowed them to unfold, and they proved to be personally meaningful as well as helpful to others.

Finally, at the end of three months, Helen heard an inner voice saying, "This is a course in miracles. Please take notes." Terrified once again that she was losing her mind, Helen resisted at first, but Bill finally convinced her to take down in shorthand the words she was hearing. Thus began a six-year collaborative process of transcribing and typing Helen's dictation—and *A Course in Miracles* was born. With its emphasis on healing, and particularly on healing relationships, the *Course* was clearly the guide to a better way of living that Helen and Bill had agreed to seek together. Since she felt she was the scribe, not the author of this material, Helen chose to remain anonymous. In her own words she said:

> *Three startling months preceded the actual writing ... Although I had grown more accustomed to the unexpected by that time, I was still very surprised when I wrote, "This is A Course in Miracles. ..." That was my introduction to the Voice. It made no sound, but seemed to be giving me a kind of rapid, inner dictation which I took down in a shorthand notebook. The writing was never automatic. It could be interrupted at any time and later picked up again. It made me very uncomfortable, but it never seriously occurred to me to stop. It seemed to be a special assignment I had somehow, somewhere agreed to complete. It represented a truly collaborative venture between my friend (William Thetford) and myself, and much of its significance, I am sure, lies in that. ... The whole process took about six years.*

The Nature of the *Course*

The *Course* itself consists of three books. The first is a text that lays out the thought system; the second is a practical workbook with a lesson for each day of the year; and the third is a teacher's manual that clarifies terms and discusses some of the principles of teaching. Two smaller booklets on psychotherapy and prayer, similarly scribed, are also available.

The language of the *Course* is traditionally Christian, reminiscent of the King James Bible. Some words and phrases sound dated, and the masculine pronoun is used exclusively. The *Course* makes no gender distinction, since in the realm of spirit, gender is transcended. However, people who initially find the language offputting may prefer to substitute terms that are more acceptable, for example, "Child of God" for "Son of God." The form of the language, therefore, need not obscure the power and beauty of the essential message. When this is realized then the poetic beauty of the language and the profound impact of the message are free to work their transformations on the reader. Indeed, the quality of writing has been compared to some of the great works in English literature and much of the *Course* is written in iambic pentameter, like Shakespearean blank verse.

The *Course* contains a wealth of succinct, powerful, and moving aphorisms that readily stand by themselves as potent capsules of wisdom. For those who have already studied the material, these quotes may provide fresh opportunities to appreciate it and offer easy access to ideas on specific subjects. For those unfamiliar with the *Course*, these quotations may introduce and stimulate interest in the original source.

Certainly a full appreciation of the *Course* demands studying the original material, whose extraordinary richness, profundity, and integrated thought system cannot possibly be represented in brief extracts. In the *Course*, thoughts build on and interweave with one another in a mutually supportive network of ideas that create a symphonic whole of which no extract, no matter how beautiful and succinct, can express more than a partial perspective. The parts cannot substitute for the whole any more than a few melodies can substitute for a symphony. The full power and impact of the *Course* can only be appreciated by studying it directly. If this book encourages readers to do so, it will have served its purpose well.

We have been studying the *Course* for several years, and our appreciation for it continues to grow. As with all profound teachings, deeper and deeper levels may be recognized as one continues to work with it. We were moved to prepare this book of aphorisms when we realized just how impactful such brief quotations could be. From among our favorites we have selected some that we consider succinct, profound, and poetic, and capable of being understood without previous familiarity with the *Course* itself.

This book is divided into three major parts. These reflect the original three separate books of quotations—*Accept This Gift, A Gift of Peace,* and *A Gift of Healing*—which have been combined into this volume. The first part offers a general introduction to the ideas of the *Course* while the other two focus on peace and healing respectively.

Peace

Has there ever been a time in human history when the need for peace was greater? Each year new wars erupt and a trillion dollars are spent on weapons, while millions of people remain hungry, helpless, and homeless.

Yet, it is not that we are any more aggressive than our predecessors. Indeed, at this very moment millions of people are devoting their lives to calming hostilities, redressing injustices, and helping the poor and deprived. Rather, advances in technological power have awesomely magnified the impact of our negative states of mind. These negative states—such as emotions of greed and anger, thoughts of attack and revenge, and misperceptions of people and situations—are the root causes of the global problems we face today. The global turmoil mirrors our own inner turmoil, and the state of the world reflects the state of our minds.

Once this is recognized it becomes apparent that our global "problems" (nuclear weapons, ecological disturbances, mass starvation, etc.) are actually symptoms; symptoms of the psychological conflicts within us and between us. The basic source of our problems, as well as of their solutions, lies within us. Therefore, only solutions that include changing our minds are likely to be effective. Yet, it is tragic how rarely this apparently obvious fact is recognized. Rather, most responses tend to be military, political, or economic and usually leave the psychological and spiritual roots of the problems untouched or even exacerbated.

The question that therefore naturally arises, and it may be one of the most important questions of our time, is this: "What can we do to treat not only the global crises but also the deep psychological roots from which these crises arise?"

The great religions have addressed these root causes of suffering throughout human history. Each culture and age has brought forth its own version of the perennial wisdom that lies at the heart of the great religions. *A Course in Miracles* represents one form of this perennial wisdom for our own time.

Peace is one of the central aims of the *Course*. It offers a road map for finding the peace for which everyone yearns, which the world so desperately needs, and which religious sages throughout the ages have called "the highest form of happiness." "Forget not," it says, "that the motivation for this course is the attainment and the keeping of the state of peace."

The peace that the *Course* would have us experience is all encompassing, embracing our hearts and minds, our relationships, and the world. It points out that we cannot hope to create a peaceful world if we ourselves are not at peace. Peace, like love, it says, must first be uncovered within and then extended through our relationships in ever-widening, ever more inclusive circles, until eventually peace encompasses everyone "without exception and without reserve." Moreover, this inner peace is not something that we create but rather something that already exists within us as part of our true identity.

Recognizing this peace and extending it in the world requires removing the obstacles—the fears and fantasies, anger and aggression, defenses and distortions—that keep our true identity from being known to us. Moreover, as we relinquish these obstacles we discover that we never really needed them in the first place. Rather we find that our true Self has no need of anger, fear, or defensiveness and is naturally loving, joyous, and peaceful. Such is a central claim of *A Course in Miracles.*

To the extent that we recognize the love, joy, and peace that constitute our true identity, to that extent we desire to extend them through sharing them. Such sharing is both the means for, and the result of removing the obstacles to the awareness of our Self and our inner peace. For *A Course in Miracles* suggests that what we give we receive, what we teach we learn, and as we see others we see ourselves. Therefore it recommends that we "learn that giving and receiving are the same," "teach peace to learn it," and "remember in your brother you but see yourself." Very simply, then, offering peace to others is a way to have it ourselves, and a natural result of having it is sharing it.

Healing

No one would deny humankind's great need for healing. All around us in this war-torn world the evidence is clear for anyone willing to see it. On a grand scale one sees wars, famine, disaster, and disease; on a small scale the countless little hurts, psychological and physical, spiritual and emotional, that we all know so well. Sickness and death, pain and sorrow, separation and loss are clearly part of our human condition. Of course, there are also periods of great love, joy, and peace, and some of us are fortunate enough to experience many of these. But even into the most fortunate lives pain intrudes at times.

Dissatisfaction with our lives, the limits of the body, and the inescapability of death have been central themes of the great religions. In the immensity of the universe we seem "as dust," say the ancient biblical psalms. Our lives are "but toil and trouble; they are soon gone. . . . they come to an end like a sigh" (Psalm 90). "What man can live and not see death?" (Psalm 89). In the "Hindu Bible," the Bhagavad Gita, the wise are said to be those capable of "seeing the defects in birth, death, old age, sickness, and suffering." "Unenlightened existence is inherently unsatisfactory," states the Buddha's First Noble Truth. Recently, this sentiment has been echoed by contemporary existentialists who see anxiety, angst, and despair as inescapable elements of human life.

But the great religions do not stop with merely recognizing the pain of our usual existence. They go further, to declare that we can escape the pain, and they offer us means for this escape.

The great religions claim that our suffering is the product of ignorance and illusion. Suffering, they say, results when we forget who we really are—Children of God, Atman, Buddha Nature, or one with the Tao—and mistake ourselves for limited beings, skin-encapsulated egos trapped inside fragile, transitory bodies. We suffer ultimately, say the great religions, from a case of mistaken identity, a false self-concept, an erroneous image that is but a pale shadow of our true limitless being. We live not in reality, but in illusion—maya or samsara. We have forgotten who we really are and misperceive our nightmares of sickness and suffering for reality, while our true nature abides unchanged and unchangeable as pure radiant sat-chit-ananda: limitless consciousness, being, and bliss.

From this viewpoint, the sickness and suffering that seem inescapable from our egocentric perspective are recognized as illusions, incapable of harming our true Self in any way. All suffering is seen as but a dream. It follows that healing sickness and pain involves awakening from our collective dream and remembering who we really are. This awakening is known in various traditions as salvation, satori, liberation, or enlightenment. It need not necessarily involve changes in our physical circumstances because our pain and sickness, and even our bodies, are part of a dream. We need not seek to change our true nature, which is actually unchangeable. Rather we need only recognize, remember, and awaken to it, and the nightmare of suffering ceases to control us. As *A Course in Miracles* says: "Those who seek the light are merely covering their eyes. The light is in them now. Enlightenment is but a recognition, not a change at all." This recognition has been the goal of spiritual teachers and traditions across countless cultures and centuries, and each has offered a path and practice by which it can occur.

Like other forms of the perennial wisdom, the *Course* recognizes the universality of pain in human existence and the universal need for healing. It therefore offers us a path of healing and awakening by which our dreams of suffering can be recognized for what they are, and our true nature can be remembered.

In offering this path, the *Course* makes a diagnosis of our condition, identifies its causes, and presents a treatment plan. It emphasizes that our dreams are perpetuated by unhealthy habits, desires, and states of mind such as fear, anger, and attack. When we let these go, says the *Course*, we awaken from the dream and recognize ourselves as we have always been: Children of God, limitless, blissful, loving, and free from suffering of any kind.

The means for this healing involves a systematic practice of mental habits that reduce and ultimately eliminate painful mind states. The *Course* encourages us to exchange anger for forgiveness, fear for love, and curse for blessing. In short, it advises us to substitute peaceful, loving states for angry, painful ones. This is no small task; countless people have devoted their lives to this aim and have found it to be a forbidding challenge. But *A Course in Miracles* claims to offer a gentle path in which this task of healing and awakening is made as easy as possible, demanding no sacrifice of any kind. For how could it be a sacrifice, asks the *Course*, to substitute the peace and joy of reality for the painful illusions of the ego?

The *Course*'s view of healing, then, is radically different from the usual views of the world. The world sees sickness and healing as originating in the body; the *Course* sees them as originating in the mind. "Sickness is of the mind," it repeats again and again. It is the mind which is really in need of healing.

From the perspective of the perennial wisdom this radical claim makes perfect sense. For if our true nature or Self remains unchanged and joyous while a mere fragment of the mind dreams of being trapped in a finite, suffering body, then an awakening of the mind is needed primarily rather than a change in the body. The *Course*, therefore, offers a path of healing for our minds that will allow us to awaken from this dream of sickness, suffering, and separation from God.

Reading This Book

This book can best be read and reread slowly and reflectively, allowing time to appreciate the feelings it evokes. Responses to the material tend to vary with different moods and circumstances. What seems difficult at one time may seem obvious at another; what feels healing at times of stress or transition may be a source of joy and delight in quiet moments of contemplation. Some people find it instructive to turn to the material with particular questions in mind, for example, "What is important for me to learn?" "How can I improve my relationships?" "What should I remember today?" "How can I learn to love more fully?" Simply holding a question in mind and opening the book at random can be surprisingly helpful.

The *Course*, therefore, is not only intellectually sophisticated but also eminently practical. To facilitate its practical application, many of the lessons contain affirmations. These are "I" statements that, if repeated to oneself, can change thinking and behavior in desired directions. Affirmations have been included at the end of most sections and are printed in italics.

A Course in Miracles has been deeply meaningful to us, and we are grateful to the Foundation for Inner Peace for allowing us to share it in this way. We hope that these selections will prove as helpful to you as they have to us, and that they will contribute to peace and healing in the world.

Accept This Gift

1
THE PATH OF LIGHT

The Nature of the Course
Miracles
Purpose
Choice
Truth and Reality

Enlightenment is but a recognition,
not a change at all.

A Course in Miracles *offers us a path of awakening. Like other paths, the* Course *suggests that our usual perception, awareness, and sense of identity are clouded and distorted. It therefore offers us a means of correcting these distortions so that we may see ourselves and the world more clearly. This transformation of perception is what the* Course *means by a "miracle."*

The Nature of the Course

This course was sent
to open up the path of light to us,
and teach us, step by step,
how to return to the eternal Self
we thought we lost.

The goal of the curriculum,
regardless of the teacher you choose,
is "Know thyself."

This is a course in mind training.

To learn this course requires willingness
to question every value that you hold.

The course does not aim at teaching
the meaning of love,
for that is beyond what can be taught.
It does aim, however, at removing the blocks
to the awareness of love's presence,
which is your natural inheritance.

Your goal is to find out who you are.

Miracles

Miracles are natural.
When they do not occur,
something has gone wrong.

Miracles are merely the translation
of denial into truth.

Miracles occur naturally as expressions of love.
The real miracle is the love that inspires them.
In this sense everything that comes from love
is a miracle.

The miracle comes quietly into the mind
that stops an instant and is still.

The miracle of life is ageless
born in time but nourished in eternity.

I offer only miracles today,
for I would have them be returned to me.

Purpose

In any situation in which you are uncertain,
the first thing to consider, very simply, is
"What do I want to come of this?
What is it *for*?"
The clarification of the goal belongs at the beginning,
for it is this which will determine the outcome.

Doubt is the result of conflicting wishes.
Be sure of what you want,
and doubt becomes impossible.

Nothing is difficult that is *wholly* desired.

No one who has a single purpose,
unified and sure,
can be afraid.
No one who shares his purpose with him
can *not* be one with him.

It is this one intent we seek today,
uniting our desires with the need of every heart,
the call of every mind,
the hope that lies beyond despair,
the love attack would hide,
the brotherhood that hate has sought to sever,
but which still remains as God created it.

The peace of God is my one goal; the aim
Of all my living here, the end I seek,
My purpose and my function and my life,
While I abide where I am not at home.

Choice

Deceive yourself no longer that you are helpless
in the face of what is done to you.
Acknowledge but that you have been mistaken,
and all effects of your mistakes will disappear.

If you choose to see yourself as unloving
you will not be happy.
You are condemning yourself
and must therefore regard yourself as inadequate.

Trials are but lessons that you failed to learn
presented once again,
so where you made a faulty choice before
you now can make a better one,
and thus escape all pain
that what you chose before
has brought to you.

It is still up to you to choose
to join with truth or with illusion.
But remember that to choose one
is to let the other go.

Pain is illusion;
joy, reality.
Pain is but sleep;
joy is awakening.
Pain is deception;
joy alone is truth.
And so again we make
the only choice that ever can be made;
we choose between illusions and the truth,
or pain and joy,
or hell and Heaven.

I am *responsible for what I see.*
I choose the feelings I experience,
and I decide upon the goal I would achieve.
And everything that seems to happen to me
I ask for and receive as I have asked.

Truth and Reality

Truth can only be experienced.
It cannot be described
and it cannot be explained.

Truth is beyond your ability to destroy,
but entirely within your ability to accept.

Do not try to look beyond yourself for truth,
for truth can only be within you.

Truth lies only in the present,
and you will find it if you seek it there.

Truth is restored to you through your desire,
as it was lost to you through your desire
for something else.

How can a fact be fearful
unless it disagrees
with what you hold more dear than truth?

The search for truth is but the honest searching out
of everything that interferes with truth.
Truth *is*.
It can neither be lost nor sought nor found.
It is there, wherever you are, being within you.
Yet it can be recognized or unrecognized.

You cannot be safe *from* truth,
but only *in* truth.
Reality is the only safety.

Merely by being what it is,
does truth release you
from everything that it is not.

Reality cannot "threaten" anything except illusions,
since reality can only uphold truth.

Nothing real can be threatened.
Nothing unreal exists.
Herein lies the peace of God.

When a situation has been dedicated
wholly to truth,
peace is inevitable.

I am in need of nothing but the truth.

2

THE MIND

Mind
Belief
Thought
Perception

There is no limit on your learning
because there is no limit on your mind.

*The source of all our experience is mind. The true nature of
mind, says the Course, is limitless transcendent awareness
and creative power. However, our mistaken thoughts and
beliefs, which direct the mind's activity, appear to distort,
constrict, and fragment it. Consequently we must change
our thoughts and beliefs in order to correct our perception
and to restore the mind to its full potential.*

Mind

Every mind contains all minds,
for every mind is one.

Whatever you accept into your mind
has reality for you.
It is your acceptance of it
that makes it real.

Release your mind,
and you will look upon a world released.

If a mind perceives without love,
it perceives an empty shell
and is unaware of the spirit within.

Minds are joined;
bodies are not.
Only by assigning to the mind
the properties of the body
does separation seem to be possible.
And it is mind that seems to be
fragmented and private and alone.

The body is a limit
imposed on the universal communication
that is an eternal property of mind.
But the communication is internal.
Mind reaches to itself.
It does not go out.
Within itself it has no limits,
and there is nothing outside it.
It encompasses you entirely;
you within it and it within you.

The mind we share is shared by all our brothers,
and as we see them truly
they will be healed.

Minds can only join in truth.
In dreams, no two can share the same intent.

The wakened mind is one that knows
its Source, its Self, its Holiness.

The mind that serves the Holy Spirit
is unlimited forever,
in all ways,
beyond the laws of time and space,
unbound by any preconceptions,
and with strength and power to do
whatever it is asked.

I rule my mind, which I alone must rule.
I have a kingdom I must rule.
At times, it does not seem I am its king at all.
It seems to triumph over me,
and tell me what to think,
and what to do and feel.
And yet it has been given me to serve
whatever purpose I perceive in it.
My mind can only serve.
Today I give its service to the Holy Spirit
to employ as He sees fit.
I thus direct my mind,
which I alone can rule.
And thus I set it free
to do the Will of God.

Belief

Your state of mind
and your recognition of what is in it
depend on what you believe about your mind.
Whatever these beliefs may be,
they are the premises that will determine
what you accept into your mind.

When you believe something,
you have made it true for you.

No belief is neutral.
Every one has the power to dictate
each decision you make.
For a decision is a conclusion
based on everything that you believe.

The recognition that you do not understand
is a prerequisite
for undoing your false ideas.

Truth will correct all errors in my mind.

Thought

There is no more self-contradictory concept
than that of "idle thoughts."
What gives rise to the perception of a whole world
can hardly be called idle.
Every thought you have
contributes to truth or to illusion;
either it extends the truth
or it multiplies illusions.

Every thought you have
makes up some segment
of the world you see.
It is with your thoughts, then,
that we must work,
if your perception of the world
is to be changed.

Nothing but your own thoughts
can hamper your progress.

Your ability to direct your thinking as you choose
is part of its power.
If you do not believe you can do this
you have denied the power of your thought,
and thus rendered it powerless in your belief.

You may believe that you are responsible
for what you do,
but not for what you think.
The truth is that you are responsible
for what you think,
because it is only at this level that
you can exercise choice.
What you do comes from what you think.

I am affected only by my thoughts.

Perception

Misperceptions produce fear
and true perceptions foster love.

You respond to what you perceive,
and as you perceive
so shall you behave.

Everything you perceive is a witness
to the thought system you want to be true.

What you perceive in others
you are strengthening in yourself.

Perception is a choice and not a fact.
But on this choice depends far more
than you may realize as yet.
For on the voice you choose to hear,
and on the sights you choose to see,
depends entirely your whole belief in what you are.

Instruction in perception is your great need.

What would you see?
The choice is given you.
But learn and do not let your mind
forget this law of seeing:
You will look upon that which you feel within.
If hatred finds a place within your heart,
you will perceive a fearful world,
held cruelly in death's sharp-pointed, bony fingers.
If you feel the Love of God within you,
you will look out on a world of mercy and of love.

Learn how to look on all things
with love, appreciation, and open-mindedness.

You have no conception of the limits
you have placed on your perception,
and no idea of all the loveliness that you could see.

Perception can make whatever picture
the mind desires to see.
Remember this.
In this lies either Heaven or hell,
as you elect.

Perception is a mirror, not a fact.
And what I look on is my state of mind,
reflected outward.

3

DREAMS AND ILLUSIONS

Dreams
Illusions

Your sleeping and your waking dreams
have different forms, and that is all.

From our sleeping dreams we learn that our minds have the
ability to create worlds that, while we remain asleep, seem
completely real and appear to be outside us. Yet all the people
and things in these dreams are actually creations of our own
minds that we mistook for objective reality. Only when we
awaken do we recognize that none of the events that seemed
to happen in the dream ever occurred.

   Like the deepest teachings of the great religions, the
Course emphasizes that what we call "reality" is also a
dream—a dream from which we have not yet awakened and
hence do not recognize. The aim of the Course is to help us
recognize our dreams and illusions and to awaken from them.

Dreams

Dreams show you that you have the power
to make a world as you would have it be,
and that because you want it you see it.
And while you see it you do not doubt that it is real.
Yet here is a world, clearly within your mind,
that seems to be outside.

What you seem to waken to is but another form
of this same world you see in dreams.
All your time is spent in dreaming.
Your sleeping and your waking dreams
have different forms, and that is all.

In dreams effect and cause are interchanged,
for here the maker of the dream
believes that what he made
is happening to him.

The miracle establishes you dream a dream,
and that its content is not true.
This is a crucial step in dealing with illusions.
No one is afraid of them
when he perceives he made them up.
The fear was held in place because he did not see
that he was author of the dream,
and not a figure in the dream.

The first change,
before dreams disappear,
is that your dreams of fear
are changed to happy dreams.

Forgiving dreams are kind
to everyone who figures in the dream.
And so they bring the dreamer full release
from dreams of fear.

Do not forget that your will has power
over all fantasies and dreams.
Trust it to see you through,
and carry you beyond them all.

Let not some dreams be more acceptable,
reserving shame and secrecy for others.
They are one. And being one,
one question should be asked of all of them,
"Is this what I would have,
in place of Heaven and the peace of God?"
This is the choice you make.
Be not deceived that it is otherwise.
No compromise is possible in this.
You choose God's peace,
or you have asked for dreams.

To mean you want the peace of God
is to renounce all dreams.
For no one means these words who wants illusions,
and who therefore seeks the means which bring illusions.
He has looked on them, and found them wanting.
Now he seeks to go beyond them,
recognizing that another dream would offer
nothing more than all the others.

The end of dreaming is the end of fear.

Now I see that I need only truth.
In that all needs are satisfied,
all cravings end,
all hopes are finally fulfilled
and dreams are gone.

Illusions

Every fantasy,
be it of love or hate,
deprives you of knowledge
for fantasies are the veil
behind which truth is hidden.
To lift the veil that seems so dark and heavy,
it is only needful to value truth beyond all fantasy,
and to be entirely unwilling to settle for illusion
in place of truth.

Every illusion carries pain and suffering
in the dark folds of the heavy garments
in which it hides its nothingness.

Freedom from illusions lies
only in not believing them.

What is temptation
but a wish to make illusions real?

One illusion cherished
and defended against the truth
makes all truth meaningless,
and all illusions real.
Such is the power of belief.

Truth does not fight against illusions,
nor do illusions fight against the truth.
Illusions battle only with themselves.

You cannot perpetuate an illusion about another
without perpetuating it about yourself.

Without illusions
there could be no fear,
no doubt
and no attack.

Illusion recognized must disappear.

The father of illusions is the belief
that they have a purpose;
that they serve a need or gratify a want.
Perceived as purposeless,
they are no longer seen.

What is there to be saved from
except illusions?

Reality brings only perfect peace.
When I am upset,
it is always because I have replaced reality
with illusions I made up.

4

THE WORLD AND TIME

The World
Time

The only aspect of time
that is eternal is *now.*

The **Course** *suggests that the world and time are creations of mind and part of our dreams. When we forget this we lose awareness of our true identity and see ourselves as limited to bodies in the temporal world. Yet we are free to seek beyond the world and time for the eternal and the changeless— already present, as the* **Course** *emphasizes, in this and every moment.*

The World

Projection makes perception.
The world you see is what you gave it,
nothing more than that.
But though it is no more than that,
it is not less.
Therefore, to you it is important.
It is the witness to your state of mind,
the outside picture of an inward condition.
As a man thinketh, so does he perceive.

The world but demonstrates an ancient truth;
you will believe that others do to you
exactly what you think you did to them.

The world cannot dictate the goal
for which you search,
unless you give it power to do so.

The world that seems to hold you prisoner
can be escaped by anyone
who does not hold it dear.

What keeps the world in chains but your beliefs?
And what can save the world except your Self?

No longer is the world our enemy,
for we have chosen that we be its Friend.

Forget not that the healing of God's Son
is all the world is for.

I am not a victim of the world I see.

Time

Time and eternity are both in your mind,
and will conflict until you perceive time
solely as a means to regain eternity.

Now is the closest approximation of eternity
that this world offers.
It is in the reality of "now,"
without past or future,
that the beginning of the appreciation
of eternity lies.
For only "now" is here.

Look lovingly upon the present,
for it holds the only things that are forever true.
All healing lies within it.

When you have learned to look on everyone
with no reference at all to the past,
either his or yours as you perceive it,
you will be able to learn from what you see *now.*

To be born again is to let the past go,
and look without condemnation upon the present.

The present is before time was,
and will be when time is no more.
In it are all things that are eternal,
and they are one.

Fear is not of the present,
but only of the past and future,
which do not exist.

Why wait for Heaven?
It is here today.
Time is the great illusion it is past
or in the future.

Here in the present is the world set free.
For as you let the past be lifted
and release the future from your ancient fears,
you find escape and give it to the world.

What time but now can truth be recognized?
The present is the only time there is.

The past is gone;
the future but imagined.
These concerns are but defenses
against present change.

Unless the past is over in my mind,
the real world must escape my sight.
For I am really looking nowhere;
seeing but what is not there.

5

MISTAKEN IDENTITY

Body
Ego
Self-Concept

The ego is only an idea
and not a fact.

The Course *maintains that we have forgotten our true iden-*
tities as creators of the dream, and constructed in its place a
false self-concept, the ego. The ego sees itself as a victim of the
world, confined to the body, alone and separated from others,
the universe, and God. To awaken from the dream means
recognizing the illusory nature of this constricted self-con-
cept and perceiving the body, not as a means of grasping at
the fleeting pleasures of the world or as a prison enclosing the
Self, but as an instrument for learning and communication.

Body

The body is a limit.
Who would seek for freedom in a body
looks for it where it cannot be found.

To accept the limits of a body
is to impose these limits
on each brother whom you see.
For you must see him as you see yourself.

The mind can be made free
when it no longer sees itself as in a body,
firmly tied to it and sheltered by its presence.

The body can but serve your purpose.
As you look on it,
so will it seem to be.

Temptation has one lesson it would teach,
in all its forms,
wherever it occurs.
It would persuade the holy Son of God he is a body,
born in what must die,
unable to escape its frailty,
and bound by what it orders him to feel.

The body is a fence
the Son of God imagines he has built,
to separate parts of his Self from other parts.

To see a body
as anything except a means of communication
is to limit your mind and to hurt yourself.

Sickness is anger taken out upon the body,
so that it will suffer pain.

Healing is the result
of using the body
solely for communication.

Forgiveness lets the body
be perceived as what it is:
a simple teaching aid,
to be laid by when learning is complete.

When the body ceases to attract you,
and when you place no value on it
as a means of getting anything,
then there will be no interference in communication
and your thoughts will be as free as God's.

Who transcends the body
has transcended limitation.

I am not a body,
I am free.
For I am still as God created me.

Ego

The ego is quite literally a fearful thought.

The ego is your belief.
The ego is a confusion in identification.

This fragment of your mind
is such a tiny part of it that,
could you but appreciate the whole,
you would see instantly
that it is like the smallest sunbeam to the sun,
or like the faintest ripple on the surface of the ocean.
In its amazing arrogance,
this tiny sunbeam has decided it is the sun;
this almost imperceptible ripple
hails itself as the ocean.
Think how alone and frightened is this little thought,
this infinitesimal illusion,
holding itself apart against the universe. . . .
Do not accept this little, fenced-off aspect as yourself.
The sun and ocean are as nothing beside what you are.

Do not be afraid of the ego.
It depends on your mind,
and as you made it by believing in it,
so you can dispel it
by withdrawing belief from it.

Only your allegiance to it
gives the ego any power over you.

The distractions of ego
may seem to interfere with your learning,
but the ego has no power to distract you
unless you give it the power to do so.

You must have noticed an outstanding characteristic
of every end that the ego has accepted as its own.
When you have achieved it,
It has not satisfied you.
That is why the ego is forced to shift ceaselessly
from one goal to another,
so that you will continue to hope
it can yet offer you something.

To hold a grievance
is to let the ego rule your mind.

No one alone can judge the ego truly.
Yet when two or more join together
in searching for truth,
the ego can no longer defend its lack of content.

Our union is therefore the way
to renounce the ego in you.
The truth in both of us
is beyond the ego.

You believe that without the ego,
all would be chaos.
Yet I assure you that without the ego,
all would be love.

If you will lay aside the ego's voice,
however loudly it may seem to call;
if you will not accept its petty gifts
that give you nothing that you really want;
if you will listen with an open mind,
that has not told you what salvation is;
then you will hear the mighty Voice of truth,
quiet in power, strong in stillness,
and completely certain in Its messages.

Self-Concept

What you think you are
is a belief to be undone.

The "self" that needs protection is not real.

Every response you make
is determined by what you think you are,
and what you want to be
is what you think you are.
What you want to be, then,
must determine every response you make.

All things you seek
to make your value greater in your sight
limit you further,
hide your worth from you,
and add another bar across the door
that leads to true awareness of your Self.

The concept of the self stands like a shield,
a silent barricade before the truth,
and hides it from your sight.
All things you see are images,
because you look on them as through a barrier
that dims your sight and warps your vision,
so that you behold nothing with clarity.

Your concept of the world depends upon
this concept of the self.
And both would go,
if either one were ever raised to doubt.

I will accept the truth of what I am,
and let my mind be wholly healed today.

6

TRUE IDENTITY

Identity
Self
Spirit

What treasure would I seek and find and keep
that can compare with my Identity?

To relinquish identification with the ego and the body is to
awaken to our true identity, says the Course. *This true iden-*
tity has remained as it always was—pure spirit—forever
changeless, peaceful, and at one with God, awaiting only our
recognition.

Identity

There is no conflict that does not entail
the single, simple question, "What am I?"

Every decision you make
stems from what you think you are,
and represents the value that you put upon yourself.

Only an illusion stands between you
and the holy Self you share.

You who perceive yourself as weak and frail,
with futile hopes and devastated dreams,
born but to die, to weep and suffer pain,
hear this:
All power is given unto you in earth and Heaven.
There is nothing that you cannot do.

You will identify with what you think
will make you safe.
Whatever it may be,
you will believe that it is one with you.
Your safety lies in truth,
and not in lies.
Love is your safety.
Fear does not exist.
Identify with love, and you are safe.
Identify with love, and you are home.
Identify with love, and find your Self.

*Let me not forget
myself is nothing,
but my Self is all.*

*I was created as the thing I seek.
I am the goal the world is searching for.*

Self

Nothing beyond yourself
can make you fearful or loving,
because nothing *is* beyond you.

Seek not outside yourself.
The search implies you are not whole within.

There is nothing outside you.
That is what you must ultimately learn.

Deep within you
is everything that is perfect,
ready to radiate through you
and out into the world.

In you is all of Heaven.

Nothing you do or think or wish or make
is necessary to establish your worth.

Light and joy and peace abide in you.

"I am as God created me."
This one thought would be enough
to save you and the world,
if you believed that it is true.

Let me remember I am one with God.
At one with all my brothers and my Self.

Spirit

Spirit is in a state of grace forever.
Your reality is only spirit.
Therefore you are in a state of grace forever.

Spirit makes use of mind
as means to find its Self-expression.
And the mind which serves the spirit
is at peace and filled with joy. . . .
Yet mind can also see itself
divorced from spirit,
and perceive itself within a body
it confuses with itself.
Without its function
then it has no peace,
and happiness is alien to its thoughts.

Your mind can be possessed by illusions,
but spirit is eternally free.

7

OBSTACLES ON THE PATH

Pain
Guilt
Fear
Anger and Attack
Judgment
Defensiveness

Fear condemns and love forgives.

If we are to escape the bondage of illusions and recognize our true identity, we must overcome the obstacles that keep us from awakening. Anger and attack, defensiveness and guilt, fear and judgment are among these. The Course *suggests that we create these obstacles out of false beliefs of unworthiness, inadequacy, and vulnerability. To relinquish them we must be willing to examine both obstacles and beliefs in the light of clear awareness, through which their illusory nature can be recognized. Only then can we experience the joy which is our natural condition.*

Pain

Pain is a sign
illusions reign
in place of truth.

Pain is a wrong perspective.
When it is experienced in any form,
it is a proof of self-deception.
It is not a fact at all.
There is no form it takes
that will not disappear if seen aright.

Nothing can hurt you
unless you give it the power to do so.

Pain is but the sign
you have misunderstood yourself.

Do you not see that all your misery
comes from the strange belief that you are powerless?

Seek not outside yourself. . . .
For all your pain comes simply from a futile search
for what you want,
insisting where it must be found.

Look about the world,
and see the suffering there.
Is not your heart willing
to bring your weary brothers rest?
They must await your own release.
They stay in chains till you are free.

Pain is the ransom
you have gladly paid
not to be free.

It is your thoughts alone
that cause you pain.
Nothing external to your mind
can hurt or injure you in any way.
There is no cause beyond yourself
that can reach down and bring oppression.
No one but yourself affects you.
There is nothing in the world
that has the power to make you ill or sad,
or weak or frail.
But it is you who have the power
to dominate all things you see
by merely recognizing what you are.

I can elect to change all thoughts that hurt.

Guilt

Love and guilt cannot coexist,
and to accept one is to deny the other.

While you feel guilty your ego is in command,
because only the ego can experience guilt.

Guilt is *always* disruptive.

Guilt is the result of attack.

The end of guilt will never come
as long as you believe there is a reason for it.
For you must learn that guilt is always totally insane,
and has no reason.

Release from guilt as you would be released.
There is no other way to look within
and see the light of love.

Guilt asks for punishment,
and its request is granted.
Not in truth,
but in the world of shadows and illusions.

The guiltless mind cannot suffer.

All salvation is escape from guilt.

Only my condemnation injures me.
Only my own forgiveness sets me free.

Fear

Fear is not justified in any form.

"There is nothing to fear."
This simply states a fact.
It is not a fact to those who believe in illusions,
but illusions are not facts.
In truth there is nothing to fear.

Fear lies not in reality,
but in the minds of children
who do not understand reality.

Only your mind can produce fear.

Attempting the mastery of fear is useless.
In fact, it asserts the power of fear
by the very assumption that it need be mastered.
The true resolution rests entirely
on mastery through love.

The need to recognize fear
and face it without disguise
is a crucial step in the undoing of the ego.

Fear itself is an appeal for help.
This is what recognizing fear really means.

Fear and attack are inevitably associated.
If only attack produces fear,
and if you see attack
as the call for help that it is,
the unreality of fear must dawn on you.
For fear *is* a call for love.

Look at what you are afraid of.
Only the anticipation will frighten you.

Under each cornerstone of fear
on which you have erected your insane system of belief,
the truth lies hidden.

Where fear has gone
there love must come,
because there are but these alternatives.
Where one appears, the other disappears.
And which you share becomes the only one you have.

Without anxiety the mind is wholly kind.

*How deceived was I
to think that what I feared
was in the world,
instead of in my mind.*

Anger and Attack

Every loving thought is true.
Everything else is an appeal for healing and help,
regardless of the form it takes.
Can anyone be justified in responding with anger
to a brother's plea for help?
No response can be appropriate
except the willingness to give it to him,
for this and only this is what he is asking for.

To the extent to which you value guilt,
to that extent will you perceive a world
in which attack is justified.
To the extent to which you recognize
that guilt is meaningless,
to that extent you will perceive
attack cannot be justified.

All anger is nothing more
than an attempt to make someone feel guilty.

Those who attack do not know they are blessed.
They attack because they believe they are deprived.
Give, therefore, of your abundance,
and teach your brothers theirs.
Do not share their illusions of scarcity,
or you will perceive yourself as lacking.

If you attack error in another,
you will hurt yourself.
You cannot know your brother
when you attack him.

You will fear what you attack.

Safety is the complete relinquishment of attack.

Because your attack thoughts will be projected,
you will fear attack.
And if you fear attack,
you must believe that you are not invulnerable.
Attack thoughts therefore make you vulnerable
in your own mind,
which is where the attack thoughts are.

Anger is *never* justified.
Attack has *no* foundation.
It is here escape from fear begins,
and will be made complete.
Here is the real world given
in exchange for dreams of terror.
For it is on this
forgiveness rests,
and is but natural.

Judgment

The choice to judge rather than to know
is the cause of the loss of peace.

You have no idea
of the tremendous release and deep peace
that comes from meeting yourself and your brothers
totally without judgment.

Judgment always imprisons
because it separates segments of reality
by the unstable scales of desire.

You who would judge reality
cannot see it,
for whenever judgment enters
reality has slipped away.

No one who loves can judge,
and what he sees is free of condemnation.

Comparison must be an ego device,
for love makes none.
Specialness always makes comparisons.
It is established by a lack seen in another,
and maintained by searching for,
and keeping clear in sight,
all lacks it can perceive.

Learn this, and learn it well,
for it is here delay of happiness is shortened
by a span of time you cannot realize.
You never hate your brother for his sins,
but only for your own.

Judgment was made to be a weapon
used against the truth.
It separates what it is being used against,
and sets it off as if it were a thing apart.
And then it makes of it
what you would have it be.
It judges what it cannot understand,
because it cannot see totality
and therefore judges falsely.

Wisdom is not judgment;
it is the relinquishment of judgment.

When I have forgiven myself
and remembered who I am,
I will bless everyone and everything I see.

Defensiveness

When you feel the need arise
to be defensive about anything,
you have identified yourself with an illusion.

It is not danger that comes
when defenses are laid down.
It is safety. It is peace.
It is joy. And it is God.

No one walks the world in armature
but must have terror striking at his heart.

Defense is frightening.
It stems from fear,
increasing fear as each defense is made.
You think it offers safety.
Yet it speaks of fear made real and terror justified.

Defenses are but foolish guardians of mad illusions.

Defenselessness is all that is required
for the truth to dawn upon our minds with certainty.

Let no defenses
but your present trust
direct the future,
and this life becomes
a meaningful encounter with the truth.

Your defenses will not work,
but you are not in danger.
You have no need of them.
Recognize this,
and they will disappear.

In my defenselessness my safety lies.

8

HEALING RELATIONSHIPS

Practicing Forgiveness
Teaching and Learning
Recognizing Your Brother
Healing and Wholeness
The Holy Relationship

All healing involves replacing fear with love.

Relationships offer unique opportunities for learning, heal-
ing, and awakening. The Course *defines healing as "to make*
whole" and offers a variety of approaches by which relation-
ships based on fear and deficiency can be transformed into
holy relationships in which the obstacles to the awareness of
love and wholeness are removed. It particularly emphasizes
forgiveness of both ourselves and others as the means by
which we can use relationships to let go of the past, with its
burden of guilt and grievances, and to awaken to the present.
Here we can establish true communication, experience love,
and recognize our true Self in each other.

Practicing Forgiveness

Ask not to be forgiven,
for this has already been accomplished.
Ask, rather, to learn how to forgive.

Forgive the world,
and you will understand
that everything that God created
cannot have an end,
and nothing He did not create is real.
In this one sentence is our course explained.

What could you want
forgiveness cannot give?
Do you want peace? Forgiveness offers it.
Do you want happiness, a quiet mind,
a certainty of purpose,
and a sense of worth and beauty
that transcends the world?
Do you want care and safety,
and the warmth of sure protection always?
Do you want a quietness that cannot be disturbed,
a gentleness that never can be hurt,
a deep, abiding comfort,
and a rest so perfect it can never be upset?
All this forgiveness offers you.

You who want peace
can find it only by complete forgiveness.

In complete forgiveness,
in which you recognize
that there is nothing to forgive,
you are absolved completely.

The real world is attained simply
by the complete forgiveness of the old.

Forgive the past and let it go, for it *is* gone.

Lift up your eyes
and look on one another in innocence
born of complete forgiveness of each other's illusions.

Those you do not forgive you fear.
And no one reaches love with fear beside him.

Forgiveness always rests upon the one who offers it.

Forgiveness takes away
what stands between your brother and yourself.
It is the wish that you be joined with him,
and not apart.

Forgiveness is the answer to attack of any kind.
So is attack deprived of its effects,
and hate is answered in the name of love.

Whom you forgive is given power
to forgive you your illusions.
By your gift of freedom is it given unto you.

As you give you will receive.

Giving and receiving are the same.

Illusions about yourself and the world are one.
That is why all forgiveness is a gift to yourself.

Forgiveness is the great need of this world,
but that is because it is a world of illusions.
Those who forgive
are thus releasing themselves from illusions,
while those who withhold forgiveness
are binding themselves to them.

He who would not forgive must judge,
for he must justify his failure to forgive.
But he who would forgive himself
must learn to welcome truth
exactly as it is.

Forgiveness is the key to happiness.
Here is the answer to your search for peace.
Here is the key to meaning
in a world that seems to make no sense.
Here is the way to safety in apparent dangers
that appear to threaten you at every turn,
and bring uncertainty to all your hopes
of ever finding quietness and peace.
Here are all questions answered;
here the end of all uncertainty ensured at last.

I let forgiveness rest upon all things,
For thus forgiveness will be given me.

Teaching and Learning

Listen silently
and learn the truth of what you really want.
No more than this will you be asked to learn.

There is no need to learn through pain.
And gentle lessons are acquired joyously,
and are remembered gladly.
What gives you happiness you want to learn
and not forget.

On your learning
depends the welfare of the world.

Everyone teaches,
and teaches all the time.
This is a responsibility you inevitably assume
the moment you accept any premise at all,
and no one can organize his life
without some thought system.
Once you have developed a thought system
of any kind,
you live by it and teach it.

The question is not whether you will teach,
for in that there is no choice.
The purpose of the course might be said
to provide you with a means of choosing
what you want to teach
on the basis of what you want to learn.

The course emphasizes that
to teach *is* to learn,
so that teacher and learner are the same.
It also emphasizes that teaching is a constant process.

Teaching and learning
are your greatest strengths now,
because they enable you to change your mind
and help others to change theirs.

Remember always that what you believe
you will teach.

"As you teach so will you learn."
If that is true, and it is true indeed,
do not forget that what you teach
is teaching you.

What you teach you strengthen in yourself
because you are sharing it.

You will not see the light,
until you offer it to all your brothers.
As they take it from your hands,
so will you recognize it as your own.

Any situation must be to you
a chance to teach others what you are,
and what they are to you.
No more than that, but also never less.

Teach no one that he is
what you would not want to be.
Your brother is the mirror
in which you see the image of yourself.

Everything you teach you are learning.
Teach only love, and learn that love is yours
and you are love.

Teach only love,
for that is what you are.

Recognizing Your Brother

When you meet anyone,
remember it is a holy encounter.
As you see him you will see yourself.
As you treat him you will treat yourself.
As you think of him you will think of yourself.
Never forget this,
for in him you will find yourself or lose yourself.

Everyone lives in you,
as you live in everyone.

Only appreciation is an appropriate response
to your brother.
Gratitude is due him for both his loving thoughts
and his appeals for help,
for both are capable of bringing love
into your awareness
if you perceive them truly.

Recognize all whom you see as brothers,
because only equals are at peace.

When you have seen your brothers as yourself
you will be released.

It will be given you to see your brother's worth
when all you want for him is peace.
And what you want for him
you will receive.

In truth you and your brother stand together,
with nothing in between.

Christ stands before you both,
each time you look upon your brother.

Dream of your brother's kindnesses
instead of dwelling in your dreams on his mistakes.
Select his thoughtfulness to dream about
instead of counting up the hurts he gave.
Forgive him his illusions, and give thanks to him
for all the helpfulness he gave.
And do not brush aside his many gifts
because he is not perfect in your dreams.

You can overlook your brother's dreams.
So perfectly can you forgive him his illusions
he becomes your savior from your dreams.

It is not up to you to change your brother,
but merely to accept him as he is.

You will never know that you are co-creator with God
until you learn that your brother
is co-creator with you.

Peace to my brother, who is one with me.
Let all the world be blessed with peace through us.

Healing and Wholeness

Every situation,
properly perceived,
becomes an opportunity to heal.

All healing is essentially the release from fear.

All healing is release from the past.

You heal a brother by recognizing his worth.

To love yourself is to heal yourself.

God cannot be remembered alone.
This is what you have forgotten.
To perceive the healing of your brother
as the healing of yourself
is thus the way to remember God.

Could you but realize for a single instant
the power of healing that the reflection of God,
shining in you,
can bring to all the world,
you could not wait
to make the mirror of your mind
clean to receive the image of
the holiness that heals the world.

We are made whole in our desire to make whole.

If you wish only to be healed, you heal.
Your single purpose makes this possible.

Healing is the effect of minds that join,
as sickness comes from minds that separate.

Those who are healed
become the instruments of healing.

To forgive is to heal.

Sickness is a defense against the truth.
I will accept the truth of what I am,
and let my mind be wholly healed today.

I am here only to be truly helpful
I am here to represent Him Who sent me.
I do not have to worry
about what to say or what to do,
because He Who sent me will direct me.
I am content to be wherever He wishes,
knowing He goes there with me.
I will be healed as I let Him teach me to heal.

The Holy Relationship

Those who have joined their brothers
have detached themselves from their belief
that their identity lies in the ego.
A holy relationship is one in which you join
with what is a part of you in truth.

An unholy relationship is based on differences,
where each one thinks
the other has what he has not. . . .
A holy relationship starts from a different premise.
Each one has looked within and seen no lack.
Accepting his completion, he would extend it
by joining with another, whole as himself.
He sees no difference between these selves,
for differences are only of the body.

You cannot know your own perfection
until you have honored
all those who were created like you.

When you have become willing to hide nothing,
you will not only be willing to enter into communion,
but will also understand peace and joy.

The Kingdom cannot be found alone,
and you who are the Kingdom
cannot find yourself alone.

There is no veil the Love of God
in us together cannot lift.

When you accepted truth
as the goal for your relationship,
you became a giver of peace.

No illusion can disturb the peace
of a relationship that has become the means of peace.

In your relationship is this world's light.

Alone we can do nothing,
but together our minds fuse into something
whose power is far beyond
the power of its separate parts.
By not being separate,
the Mind of God is established in ours and as ours.
This Mind is invincible because it is undivided.

You are one Self with me,
United with our Creator in this Self.
I honor you because of what I am,
And what He is, Who loves us both as one.

9

THE PEACEFUL ALTERNATIVE

Coming Home
Freedom
Salvation
Love
Awakening to God
The Conditions of Peace
Light and Joy

Peace is the state where love abides,
and seeks to share itself.

Only when the mind is at peace can it be freed of illusions
and opened to the liberating influence of love, joy, and the
memory of God that lie deep within us. In this experience we
regain our sanity, salvation, and Self.

Coming Home

Would you not go through fear to love?
For such the journey seems to be.

It is a journey without distance
to a goal that has never changed.

You dwell not here,
but in eternity.
You travel but in dreams,
while safe at home.

There is no journey,
but only an awakening.

You are coming home together,
after a long and meaningless journey
that you undertook apart,
and that led nowhere.
You have found your brother,
and you will light each other's ways.

I will be still an instant and go home.

Freedom

It is essential that you free yourself quickly,
because you must emerge from the conflict
if you are to bring peace to other minds.

Hold no one prisoner.
Release instead of bind,
for thus are you made free.

You are not free to give up freedom,
but only to deny it.

As long as a single "slave" remains to walk the earth,
your release is not complete.

Be free today.
And carry freedom as your gift
to those who still believe
they are enslaved within a body.
Be you free,
so that the Holy Spirit
can make use of your escape from bondage,
to set free the many who perceive themselves
as bound and helpless and afraid.
Let love replace their fears through you.

I give you to the Holy Spirit as part of myself.
I know that you will be released, unless I want to
use you to imprison myself.
In the name of my freedom I choose your release.
Because I recognize that we will be released together.

Salvation

Changing concepts is salvation's task.

Be glad indeed salvation asks
so little, not so much.
It asks for nothing in reality.
And even in illusions it but asks
forgiveness be the substitute for fear.

Salvation is undoing.

Salvation can be seen
as nothing more
than the escape from concepts.

Those who would let illusions
be lifted from their minds
are this world's saviors.

Salvation comes from my one Self.

Love

Love will enter immediately
into any mind that truly wants it,
but it must want it truly.

Your task is not to seek for love,
but merely to seek and find
all of the barriers within yourself
that you have built against it.

Love waits on welcome,
not on time.

When you want only love
you will see nothing else.

If love is sharing,
how can you find it except through itself?
Offer it and it will come to you,
because it is drawn to itself.
But offer attack and love will remain hidden,
for it can live only in peace.

It is the nature of love to look upon only the truth,
for there it sees itself.

With love in you,
you have no need except to extend it.

You will not be able to give love welcome separately.
You could no more know God alone
than He knows you without your brother.
But together you could no more be unaware of love
than love could know you not,
or fail to recognize itself in you.

Grace is acceptance of the Love of God
within a world of seeming hate and fear.

Gratitude goes hand in hand with love,
and where one is the other must be found.

Love without trust is impossible.

Love would ask you
to lay down all defense
as merely foolish.

No course whose purpose is to teach
you to remember what you really are
could fail to emphasize that there can never be
a difference in what you really are and what love is.

If you achieve the faintest glimmering
of what love means today,
you have advanced in distance without measure
and in time beyond the count of years
to your release.

See the Love of God in you,
and you will see it everywhere
because it *is* everywhere.

Love, Which created me, is what I am.

Awakening to God

The memory of God can dawn only in a mind
that chooses to remember,
and that has relinquished the insane desire
to control reality.
You who cannot even control yourself
should hardly aspire to control the universe.

All that is needful is to train our minds
to overlook all little senseless aims,
and to remember that our goal is God.

The recognition of God
is the recognition of yourself.

God dwells within.

God's Will for you is perfect happiness.

The journey to God is merely the reawakening
of the knowledge of where you are always,
and what you are forever.

We practice but an ancient truth
we knew before illusion seemed to claim the world.
And we remind the world that it is free
of all illusions every time we say:
"God is but Love, and therefore so am I."

The Conditions of Peace

Peace is inevitable
to those who offer peace.

Peace is an attribute *in* you.
You cannot find it outside.

When the wish for peace is genuine,
the means for finding it is given
in a form each mind that seeks for it
in honesty can understand.
Whatever form the lesson takes is planned for him
in such a way that he cannot mistake it,
if his asking is sincere.
But if he asks without sincerity,
there is no form in which the lesson
will meet with acceptance
and be truly learned.

"I want the peace of God."
To say these words is nothing.
But to mean these words is everything.

The mind which means that all it wants is peace
must join with other minds,
for that is how peace is obtained.

The only way to have peace
is to teach peace.

Do you not think the world needs peace
as much as you do?
Do you not want to give it to the world
as much as you want to receive it?
For unless you do, you will not receive it.

When you have accepted your mission
to extend peace
you will find peace,
for by making it manifest you will see it.

Remember that you came
to bring the peace of God into the world.

If peace is the condition of truth and sanity,
and cannot be without them,
where peace is they must be.

The memory of God comes to the quiet mind.
It cannot come where there is conflict,
for a mind at war against itself
remembers not eternal gentleness.

When the light comes at last
into the mind given to contemplation;
or when the goal is finally achieved by anyone,
it always comes with just one happy realization:
"I need do nothing."

Those who believe that peace can be defended,
and that attack is justified on its behalf,
cannot perceive it lies within them.

Those who offer peace to everyone
have found a home in Heaven
the world cannot destroy.
For it is large enough to hold the world
within its peace.

No one who truly seeks the peace of God
can fail to find it.
For he merely asks that he deceive himself no longer
by denying to himself what is God's Will.
Who can remain unsatisfied
who asks for what he has already?

The peace of God is shining in you now,
and in all living things.
In quietness is it acknowledged universally.

The peace of God is shining in me now.
Let all things shine upon me in that peace.
And let me bless them with the light in me.

Light and Joy

You are the light of the world.

The light is *in* you.
Darkness can cover it,
but cannot put it out.

Why wait for Heaven?
Those who seek the light
are merely covering their eyes.
The light is in them now.
Enlightenment is but a recognition,
not a change at all.

There is no difference
between love and joy.

Joy has no cost.
It is your sacred right.

You can exchange all suffering
for joy this very day.
Practice in earnest,
and the gift is yours.

Forgiveness is my function
as the light of the world.

My brother, peace and joy I offer you,
That I may have God's peace and joy as mine.

10

A NEW BEGINNING

There will come a time
when images have all gone by,
and you will see you know not what you are.
It is to this unsealed and open mind
that truth returns, unhindered and unbound.
Where concepts of the Self have been laid by
is truth revealed exactly as it is.

Let us be still an instant, and forget
all things we ever learned, all thoughts we had,
and every preconception that we hold
of what things mean and what their purpose is.
Let us remember not our own ideas
of what the world is for.
We do not know.
Let every image held of everyone
be loosened from our minds and swept away.
Be innocent of judgment,
unaware of any thoughts of evil or of good
that ever crossed your mind of anyone.
Now do you know him not.
But you are free to learn of him,
and learn of him anew.

Only be quiet.
You will need no rule but this,
to let your practicing today
lift you above the thinking of the world,
and free your vision from the body's eyes.
Only be still and listen.

Simply do this:
Be still, and lay aside all thoughts
of what you are and what God is;
all concepts you have learned about the world;
all images you hold about yourself.
Empty your mind of everything
it thinks is either true or false,
or good or bad,
of every thought it judges worthy,
and all the ideas of which it is ashamed.
Hold on to nothing.
Do not bring with you one thought
the past has taught, nor one belief
you ever learned before from anything.
Forget this world,
forget this course,
and come with wholly empty hands unto your God.

A Gift of Peace

1

THE CHOICE IS OURS

A Course in Miracles teaches that our choices and desires determine the nature and quality of our experience, behavior, relationships, and ultimately even our sense of identity. Moment by moment we choose whether to feel love or hate, whether to attack or forgive, whether to see truth or illusion. Each choice determines our perception of the meaning and purpose of our lives, and each choice is a decision for or against peace.

Peace will come to all who ask for it
with real desire and sincerity of purpose.

Deciding for Peace

This world will change through you.
No other means can save it.

Do you not think the world needs peace
as much as you do?
Do you not want to give it to the world
as much as you want to receive it?
For unless you do,
you will not receive it.

The question, "What do you want?"
must be answered.
You are answering it every minute
and every second,
and each moment of decision is a judgment
that is anything but ineffectual.
Its effects will follow automatically
until the decision is changed.

The power of decision is all that is yours.
What you can decide between is fixed,
because there are no alternatives
except truth and illusion.
And there is no overlap between them,
because they are opposites
which cannot be reconciled
and cannot both be true.
You are guilty or guiltless,
bound or free,
unhappy or happy.

What could you choose between
but life or death,
waking or sleeping,
peace or war,
your dreams or your reality?

Remember this: Every decision you make
stems from what you think you are,
and represents the value that
you put upon yourself.

Yet what you do not realize,
each time you choose,
is that your choice is your evaluation of yourself.

Every response you make
is determined by what you think you are,
and what you want to be
is what you think you are.
What you want to be, then,
must determine every response you make.

The power of your wanting
must first be recognized.
You must accept its strength, and not its weakness.
You must perceive that what is strong enough
to make a world can let it go,
and can accept correction
if it is willing to see that it was wrong.

Watch carefully and see what it is
you are really asking for.
Be very honest with yourself in this,
for we must hide nothing from each other.

Make, then, your choice.
But recognize that in this choice
the purpose of the world you see is chosen.

We choose again,
and make our choice for all our brothers,
knowing they are one with us.

This day I choose to spend in perfect peace.

The power of decision is my own.

Our Shared Purpose

"What for?"
This is the question that *you* must learn to ask
in connection with everything.
What is the purpose?
Whatever it is,
it will direct your efforts automatically.
When you make a decision of purpose,
then, you have made a decision
about your future effort;
a decision that will remain in effect
unless you change your mind.

Purpose is of the mind.
And minds can change as they desire.

Those who share a purpose have a mind as one.

The power of our joint motivation is beyond belief,
but not beyond accomplishment.
What we can accomplish together has no limits.

You will see your value
through your brother's eyes,
and each one is released as he beholds his savior
in place of the attacker whom he thought was there.
Through this releasing is the world released.
This is your part in bringing peace.
For you have asked what is your function here,
and have been answered.
Seek not to change it, nor to substitute another goal.
Accept this one and serve it willingly.

The goal is clear,
but now you need specific methods for attaining it.
The speed by which it can be reached
depends on this one thing alone;
your willingness to practice every step.
Each one will help a little,
every time it is attempted.
And together will these steps
lead you from dreams of judgment
to forgiving dreams and out of pain and fear.

We have a mission here.
We did not come to reinforce the madness
that we once believed in.
Let us not forget the goal that we accepted.
It is more than just our happiness alone
we came to gain.

Let me remember what my purpose is.

2

CHANGING YOUR MIND ABOUT YOUR MIND

Although the mind's natural state is one of peace, for most of us this peace lies hidden beneath the distorting veils of faulty perceptions, thoughts, and beliefs. Peace has become something that must be rediscovered and remembered through training the mind to correct its distortions. *A Course in Miracles* emphasizes that "an undisciplined mind can accomplish nothing" and that "this is a course in mind training." Only by training the mind to correct distorted thoughts and perceptions can the gift of peace be experienced.

> *Peace of mind is clearly an internal matter.*
> *It must begin with your own thoughts,*
> *and then extend outward.*
> *It is from your peace of mind*
> *that a peaceful perception of the world arises.*

The Power of Mind

Your mind is the means
by which you determine your own condition,
because mind is the mechanism of decision.

You must learn to change your mind
about your mind.

Only your mind can produce fear.
It does so whenever it is conflicted in what it wants,
producing inevitable strain
because wanting and doing are discordant.

Only the mind can value,
and only the mind decides
on what it would receive and give.
And every gift it offers
depends on what it wants.

The world is nothing in itself.
Your mind must give it meaning.

You want to be happy.
You want peace.
You do not have them now,
because your mind is totally undisciplined.

Try to identify with the part of your mind
where stillness and peace reign forever.

Listen in deep silence.
Be very still and open your mind . . .
Sink deep into the peace that waits for you
beyond the frantic, riotous thoughts
and sights and sounds of this insane world.

There is a place in you
where there is perfect peace.
There is a place in you
where nothing is impossible.

The mind that serves spirit *is* invulnerable.

The mind which serves the spirit
is at peace and filled with joy.
Its power comes from spirit,
and it is fulfilling happily its function here.
Yet mind can also see itself divorced from spirit,
and perceive itself within a body
it confuses with itself.
Without its function then it has no peace,
and happiness is alien to its thoughts.

A tranquil mind is not a little gift.

Merely rest, alert but with no strain,
and let your mind in quietness be changed
so that the world is freed, along with you.

The mind which means that all it wants is peace
must join with other minds,
for that is how peace is obtained.
And when the wish for peace is genuine,
the means for finding it is given,
in a form each mind that seeks for it in honesty
can understand.

Alone we can do nothing,
but together our minds fuse into something
whose power is far beyond
the power of its separate parts.

Peace to my mind.
Let all my thoughts be still.

Perception Is a Mirror

You respond to what you perceive,
and as you perceive so shall you behave.

Every response you make
to everything you perceive
is up to you,
because your mind determines
your perception of it.

You cannot be aware without interpretation,
for what you perceive *is* your interpretation.

Understand that you do not respond
to anything directly,
but to your interpretation of it.
Your interpretation thus becomes
the justification for the response.

Perception selects, and makes the world you see.
It literally picks it out as the mind directs.
The laws of size and shape and brightness
would hold, perhaps,
if other things were equal.
They are not equal.
For what you look for
you are far more likely to discover
than what you would prefer to overlook.

The world can teach no images of you
unless you want to learn them.

Reality needs no cooperation from you to be itself.
But your awareness of it needs your help.

Perception is a choice
of what you want yourself to be;
the world you want to live in,
and the state in which you think your mind
will be content and satisfied.
It chooses where you think your safety lies,
at your decision.
It reveals yourself to you as you would have you be.
And always is it faithful to your purpose.

Let us be glad that you will see what you believe,
and that it has been given you to change
what you believe.

If you perceive truly
you are canceling out misperceptions
in yourself and in others simultaneously.
Because you see them as they are,
you offer them your acceptance of their truth
so they can accept it for themselves.

Let us not rest content
until the world has joined our changed perception.
Let us not be satisfied
until forgiveness has been made complete.

As I share the peace of the world with my brothers,
I begin to understand
that this peace comes from deep within myself.

122

The Power of Thought

Everything you see is the result of your thoughts.
There is no exception to this fact.

Every thought you have
brings either peace or war;
either love or fear.

From insane wishes comes an insane world.
From judgment comes a world condemned.
And from forgiving thoughts
a gentle world comes forth.

What you must recognize is
that when you do not share a thought system,
you are weakening it.
Those who believe in it
therefore perceive this as an attack on them.
This is because everyone identifies himself
with his thought system,
and every thought system centers
on what you believe you are.

You are free to believe what you choose,
and what you do attests to what you believe.

Let me look on the world I see
as the representation of my own state of mind.
I know that my state of mind can change,
and so I also know the world I see can change as well.

I have no neutral thoughts.

3

CHANGING WHAT YOU THINK IS REAL

The power of the mind is such that it can create whole worlds that appear to be real and outside us. This is most obvious in our sleeping dreams, which seem completely real to us when we are dreaming them. Only when we awaken do we recognize that all the people and things in the dream, including our own body, were actually created by our sleeping mind.

The *Course* suggests that the same is true of our usual waking state. It, too, is a dream from which we have not yet awakened. To awaken requires recognizing our dreams and illusions for what they really are and then being willing to relinquish them. In relinquishing our dreams we find reality and in reality we find peace.

Reality cannot "threaten" anything except illusions, since reality can only uphold truth.

Dreaming

Where are dreams but in a mind asleep?

You choose your dreams,
for they are what you wish,
perceived as if it had been given you.

You will first dream of peace,
and then awaken to it.
Your first exchange of what you made
for what you want
is the exchange of nightmares
for the happy dreams of love.

You recognize from your own experience
that what you see in dreams you think is real
while you are asleep.
Yet the instant you waken you realize
that everything that seemed to happen in the dream
did not happen at all.
You do not think this strange,
even though all the laws of what you awaken to
were violated while you slept.
Is it not possible that you merely shifted
from one dream to another,
without really waking?

Nothing in the world of dreams remains
without the hope of change and betterment,
for here is not where changelessness is found.
Let us be glad indeed that this is so,
and seek not the eternal in this world.
Forgiving dreams are means to step aside
from dreaming of a world outside yourself.
And leading finally beyond all dreams,
unto the peace of everlasting life.

Let forgiveness rest upon your dreams,
and be restored to sanity and peace of mind.
Without forgiveness will your dreams
remain to terrify you.

You cannot dream some dreams
and wake from some,
for you are either sleeping or awake.
And dreaming goes with only one of these.
The dreams you think you like
would hold you back
as much as those in which the fear is seen.

Escape depends, not on the dream,
but only on awaking.

Take time today to slip away from dreams
and into peace.

The Cost of Illusions

Illusions are not fearful because they are not true.
They but seem to be fearful to the extent to which
you fail to recognize them for what they are;
and you will fail to do this to the extent to which
you *want* them to be true.

Illusions are investments.
They will last as long as you value them. . . .
The only way to dispel illusions
is to withdraw all investment from them.

Projection makes perception,
and you cannot see beyond it.
Again and again have you attacked your brother,
because you saw in him
a shadow figure in your private world.

You attack in the present in retaliation
for a past that is no more.
And this decision is one of future pain.
Unless you learn that past pain is an illusion,
you are choosing a future of illusions
and losing the many opportunities you could find
for release in the present.

Every illusion is an assault on truth.

Every illusion is one of fear,
whatever form it takes.

You have paid very dearly for your illusions
and nothing you have paid for brought you peace.

As long as the illusion of hatred lasts,
so long will love be an illusion to you.
And then the only choice remaining possible
is which illusion you prefer.

Without illusions conflict is impossible.
Let us try to recognize this today,
and experience the peace this recognition brings.

Release your brothers
from the slavery of their illusions
by forgiving them for the illusions
you perceive in them.

Forget not, when you feel the need arise
to be defensive about anything,
you have identified yourself with an illusion.
And therefore feel that you are weak
because you are alone.
This is the cost of all illusions.
Not one but rests on the belief
that you are separate.

This world is but the dream that you can be alone,
and think without affecting those apart from you.

Illusions of despair may seem to come,
but learn how not to be deceived by them.
Behind each one there is reality and there is God.

Can you imagine what a state of mind
without illusions is?
How it would feel?
Try to remember when there was a time—
perhaps a minute, maybe even less—
when nothing came to interrupt your peace;
when you were certain you were loved and safe.
Then try to picture what it would be like
to have that moment be extended
to the end of time and to eternity.
Then let the sense of quiet that you felt
be multiplied a hundred times,
and then be multiplied another hundred more.
And now you have a hint,
not more than just the faintest intimation
of the state your mind will rest in
when the truth has come.

Letting Go of the Past

All healing is release from the past.

Let us forget the purpose of the world
the past has given it.
For otherwise, the future will be like the past,
and but a series of depressing dreams.

Only the past can separate,
and it is nowhere.

Your past was made in anger,
and if you use it to attack the present,
you will not see the freedom that the present holds.

There is no fantasy that does not contain
the dream of retribution for the past.
Would you act out the dream, or let it go?

The past is nothing.
Do not seek to lay the blame
for deprivation on it,
for the past is gone.

Dwell not upon the past today.
Keep a completely open mind,
washed of all past ideas
and clean of every concept you have made.
You have forgiven the world today.
You can look upon it now
as if you never saw it before.

The past is gone,
and with its passing
the drive for vengeance has been uprooted
and has disappeared.
The stillness and the peace of *now*
enfold you in perfect gentleness.
Everything is gone except the truth.

Free of the past,
you see that love is in you.

Take this very instant, now,
and think of it as all there is of time.
Nothing can reach you here out of the past,
and it is here that you are completely absolved,
completely free and wholly without condemnation.

Fear is not of the present,
but only of the past and future,
which do not exist.
There is no fear in the present
when each instant stands clear
and separated from the past,
without its shadow reaching out into the future.

The present offers you your brothers
in the light that would unite you with them,
and free you from the past.
Would you, then, hold the past against them?
For if you do,
you are choosing to remain in the darkness
that is not there,
and refusing to accept the light
that is offered you.

The present extends forever.
It is so beautiful and so clean and free of guilt
that nothing but happiness is there.
No darkness is remembered,
and immortality and joy are now.

It is enough to heal the past
and make the future free.
It is enough to let the present
be accepted as it is.

Be very still an instant.
Come without all thought
of what you ever learned before,
and put aside all images you made.
The old will fall away before the new
without your opposition or intent.

Can you imagine what it means
to have no cares, no worries, no anxieties,
but merely to be perfectly calm
and quiet all the time?
Yet that is what time is for.

Faith in the eternal is always justified,
for the eternal is forever kind,
infinite in its patience and wholly loving.
It will accept you wholly, and give you peace.
Yet it can unite only
with what already is at peace in you.

Heaven is here.
There is nowhere else.
Heaven is now.
There is no other time.

Welcoming Reality

Real freedom depends on welcoming reality.

You do not have to seek reality.
It will seek you and find you
when you meet its conditions.

You cannot distort reality and know what it is.
And if you do distort reality you will experience
anxiety, depression and ultimately panic,
because you are trying to make yourself unreal.
When you feel these things,
do not try to look beyond yourself for truth,
for truth can only be within you.

It is not the reality of your brothers
or your Father or yourself that frightens you.
You do not know what they are,
and so you perceive them as ghosts
and monsters and dragons.

How does one overcome illusions?
Surely not by force or anger,
nor by opposing them in any way.
Merely by letting reason tell you
that they contradict reality.
They go against what must be true.
The opposition comes from them,
and not reality.
Reality opposes nothing.
What merely is needs no defense,
and offers none.
Only illusions need defense because of weakness.

Only reality is free of pain.
Only reality is free of loss.
Only reality is wholly safe.
And it is only this we seek today.

4

THE OBSTACLES
TO PEACE

We usually think of other people and outside events
as the major obstacles to our peace. The *Course,* on the
other hand, emphasizes that the major obstacles to
peace reside within us as the emotions, thoughts, and
beliefs that agitate our minds, cloud our perception,
and distort our relationships. These barriers include
emotions of fear and guilt, thoughts of judgment and
condemnation, and mistaken beliefs in our specialness
and in the value of sacrifice. We find peace when we
release these emotions and question these beliefs, replacing fear and sacrifice with love and forgiveness.

> *Every obstacle that peace must flow across*
> *is surmounted in just the same way;*
> *the fear that raised it*
> *yields to the love beyond,*
> *and so the fear is gone.*

The Pursuit of Specialness

The pursuit of specialness
is always at the cost of peace.

You are not special.
If you think you are,
and would defend your specialness
against the truth of what you really are,
how can you know the truth?

Specialness always makes comparisons.
It is established by a lack seen in another,
and maintained by searching for,
and keeping clear in sight,
all lacks it can perceive.

When peace is not with you entirely,
and when you suffer pain of any kind,
you have beheld some sin within your brother,
and have rejoiced at what you thought was there.
Your specialness seemed safe because of it.

The pursuit of specialness
must bring you pain.

Forgiveness is the end of specialness.
Only illusions can be forgiven,
and then they disappear.
Forgiveness is release from all illusion.

The Meaning of Sacrifice

The first illusion, which must be displaced
before another thought system can take hold,
is that it is a sacrifice
to give up the things of this world.
What could this be but an illusion,
since this world itself is nothing more than that?

Learn now that sacrifice of any kind
is nothing but a limitation imposed on giving.

Your confusion of sacrifice and love is so profound
that you cannot conceive of love without sacrifice.
And it is this that you must look upon;
sacrifice is attack, not love.
If you would accept but this one idea,
your fear of love would vanish.

You who believe that sacrifice is love
must learn that sacrifice is separation from love.
For sacrifice brings guilt
as surely as love brings peace.

It is not love that asks a sacrifice.
But fear demands the sacrifice of love,
for in love's presence fear cannot abide.

Let us join
in celebrating peace
by demanding
no sacrifice of anyone.

The Veil of Fear and Guilt

The first obstacle that peace must flow across
is your desire to get rid of it.
For it cannot extend unless you keep it.
You are the center from which it radiates outward,
to call the others in.
You are its home; its tranquil dwelling place
from which it gently reaches out,
but never leaving you.

If you are wholly free of fear of any kind,
and if all those who meet or even think of you
share your perfect peace,
then you can be sure
that you have learned God's lesson,
and not your own.

If you are fearful,
it is certain that you will endow the world
with attributes that it does not possess,
and crowd it with images that do not exist.

Truth is eclipsed by fear,
and what remains is but imagined.

Fear is a judgment never justified.
Its presence has no meaning but to show
you wrote a fearful script,
and are afraid accordingly.

Look at what you are afraid of.
Only the anticipation will frighten you.

How weak is fear;
how little and how meaningless.
How insignificant before the quiet strength
of those whom love has joined.

The journey that we undertake together
is the exchange of dark for light,
of ignorance for understanding.
Nothing you understand is fearful.

We go beyond the veil of fear,
lighting each other's way.

What is fear except love's absence?

Step back from fear,
and make advance to love.

Fear binds the world.
Forgiveness sets it free.

As love must look past fear,
so must fear see love not.
For love contains the end of guilt,
as surely as fear depends on it.

You think you hold against your brother
what he has done to you.
But what you really blame him for
is what *you* did to *him.*
It is not his past but yours
you hold against him.
And you lack faith in him
because of what you were.

Those whom you see as guilty
become the witnesses to guilt in you.

If you did not feel guilty
you could not attack,
for condemnation is the root of attack.
It is the judgment of one mind by another
as unworthy of love and deserving of punishment.

In any union with a brother
in which you seek to lay your guilt upon him,
or share it with him or perceive his own,
you will feel guilty.

Peace and guilt are antithetical.

The end of guilt will never come
as long as you believe there is a reason for it.
For you must learn
that guilt is always totally insane.

It is impossible to use one relationship
at the expense of another and not to suffer guilt.
And it is equally impossible
to condemn part of a relationship
and find peace within it.

Ask yourself honestly,
"Would I want to have perfect communication,
and am I wholly willing
to let everything that interferes with it go forever?"

Where there is communication
there is peace.

It is as sure that those who hold grievances
will suffer guilt,
as it is certain that those who forgive
will find peace.

Do not be afraid to look within.
The ego tells you
all is black with guilt within you,
and bids you not to look.
Instead, it bids you look upon your brothers,
and see the guilt in them.
Yet this you cannot do without remaining blind.

Only in your guiltlessness can you be happy.

Release from guilt as you would be released.

Fear is simply a mistake.
Let me not be afraid of truth today.

Releasing Judgment and Defense

The strain of constant judgment
is virtually intolerable.
It is curious that an ability so debilitating
would be so deeply cherished.

When you recognize what you are
and what your brothers are,
you will realize that judging them in any way
is without meaning. In fact,
their meaning is lost to you
precisely *because* you are judging them.

See yourself without condemnation,
by learning how to look on everything without it.

Instead of judging,
we need but be still
and let all things be healed.

Judgment and love are opposites.
From one come all the sorrows of the world.
But from the other comes the peace of God.

No one who loves can judge,
and what he sees is free of condemnation.

Judge not,
for you but judge yourself.

Those who believe that peace can be defended,
and that attack is justified on its behalf,
cannot perceive it lies within them.

Anger makes attack seem reasonable,
honestly provoked, and righteous
in the name of self-defense.
Yet is defensiveness a double threat.
For it attests to weakness,
and sets up a system of defense that cannot work.

A defense that cannot attack
is the best defense.

Truth has a power far beyond defense,
for no illusions can remain
where truth has been allowed to enter.
And it comes to any mind
that would lay down its arms,
and cease to play with folly.
It is found at any time;
today, if you will choose to practice
giving welcome to the truth.
This is our aim today.

Today we learn a lesson
which can save you more delay
and needless misery than you can possibly imagine.
It is this:
You make what you defend against, and by
Your own defense against it, is it real
And inescapable. Lay down your arms,
And only then do you perceive it false.

Help is here.
Learn to be quiet in the midst of turmoil,
for quietness is the end of strife
and this is the journey to peace.

How strong is he who comes without defenses,
offering only love's messages
to those who think he is their enemy.

If I defend myself I am attacked.
But in defenselessness I will be strong,
And I will learn what my defenses hide.

5

THE END OF CONFLICT

Conflict and war in the world reflect conflict and war in the mind, and both this inner and outer turmoil are born of thoughts of anger and attack. The relinquishment of anger and attack and the practice of forgiveness are, therefore, essential to the realization of peace both in the world and in ourselves.

Forgiveness ends the dream of conflict.

Reinterpreting Anger and Attack

Perhaps it will be helpful to remember
that no one can be angry at a fact.
It is always an interpretation
that gives rise to negative emotions,
regardless of their seeming justification
by what *appears* as facts.

If anger comes from an interpretation and not a fact,
it is never justified.
Once this is even dimly grasped,
the way is open.

When you are angry,
is it not because someone has failed
to fill the function you allotted him?
And does not this become the "reason"
your attack is justified?

Without projection there can be no anger,
but it is also true that without extension
there can be no love.

Accept only loving thoughts in others
and regard everything else as an appeal for help.

There is nothing to prevent you from recognizing
all calls for help as exactly what they are
except your own imagined need to attack.

If you attack error in another,
you will hurt yourself.
You cannot know your brother
when you attack him.
Attack is always made upon a stranger.
You are making him a stranger
by misperceiving him,
and so you cannot know him.
It is because you have made him a stranger
that you are afraid of him.
Perceive him correctly so that you can know him.

Because your attack thoughts will be projected,
you will fear attack.

Projection and attack are inevitably related,
because projection is always
a means of justifying attack.
Anger without projection is impossible.

Any concept of punishment
involves the projection of blame,
and reinforces the idea that blame is justified.
The result is a lesson in blame,
for all behavior teaches the beliefs that motivate it.

Those whom you perceive as opponents
are part of your peace,
which you are giving up by attacking them.

Safety is the complete relinquishment of attack.
No compromise is possible in this.
Teach attack in any form and you have learned it,
and it will hurt you.

The strong do not attack
because they see no need to do so.
Before the idea of attack can enter your mind,
you must have perceived yourself as weak.

Everyone here has entered darkness,
yet no one has entered it alone.
For he has come with Heaven's Help within him,
ready to lead him out of darkness
into light at any time.
The time he chooses can be any time,
for help is there, awaiting but his choice.
And when he chooses to avail himself
of what is given him,
then will he see each situation
that he thought before was means
to justify his anger
turned to an event which justifies his love.
He will hear plainly that the calls to war
he heard before are really calls to peace.
He will perceive that where he gave attack
is but another altar where he can,
with equal ease and far more happiness,
bestow forgiveness.
And he will reinterpret all temptation
as just another chance to bring him joy.

Joy goes with gentleness
as surely as grief attends attack.

The perfectly safe are wholly benign.
They bless because they know that they are blessed.

Today we . . . take a stand against our anger,
that our fears may disappear
and offer room to love.

153

Grievances are completely alien to love.
Grievances attack love and keep its light obscure.
If I hold grievances I am attacking love,
and therefore attacking my Self.

Without attack thoughts
I could not see a world of attack.
As forgiveness allows love
to return to my awareness,
I will see a world of peace and safety and joy.
And it is this I choose to see,
in place of what I look on now.

The Resolution of Conflict and War

Conflict is sleep, and peace awakening.

There must be doubt before there can be conflict.
And every doubt must be about yourself.

It is only the wish to deceive that makes war.
No one at one with himself
can even conceive of conflict.
Conflict is the inevitable result of self-deception,
and self-deception is dishonesty.

War is the condition in which fear is born,
and grows and seeks to dominate.
Peace is the state where love abides,
and seeks to share itself.
Conflict and peace are opposites.
Where one abides the other cannot be;
where either goes the other disappears.
So is the memory of God obscured in minds
that have become illusions' battleground.
Yet far beyond this senseless war it shines,
ready to be remembered when you side with peace.

Only the trusting can afford honesty,
for only they can see its value.
Honesty does not apply only to what you say.
The term actually means consistency.
There is nothing you say that contradicts
what you think or do;
no thought opposes any other thought;
no act belies your word;
and no word lacks agreement with another.
Such are the truly honest.
At no level are they in conflict with themselves.
Therefore it is impossible for them
to be in conflict with anyone or anything.

In quietness are all things answered,
and is every problem quietly resolved.
In conflict there can be no answer and no resolution,
for its purpose is to make no resolution possible,
and to ensure no answer will be plain.
A problem set in conflict has no answer,
for it is seen in different ways.
And what would be an answer
from one point of view
is not an answer in another light.

The conflict of illusions disappears
when it is brought to truth!
For it seems real only as long as it is seen
as war between conflicting truths . . .
Conflict is the choice between illusions,
one to be crowned as real,
the other vanquished and despised.

Illusions are but beliefs in what is not there.
And the seeming conflict between truth and illusion
can only be resolved by separating yourself
from the illusion and not the truth.

Illusion meets illusion; truth, itself.
The meeting of illusions leads to war.
Peace, looking on itself, extends itself.

I must have decided wrongly,
because I am not at peace.
I made the decision myself,
but I can also decide otherwise.
I want to decide otherwise,
because I want to be at peace.

6

PEACE TO MY BROTHER, WHO IS ONE WITH ME

A Course in *Miracles* suggests that we suffer from a case of mistaken identity. We have forgotten our true Self, which is said to be limitless, transcendent, and eternal. Instead we regard ourselves as an ego or separate self, limited to the body, fragile, ephemeral, and vulnerable. We therefore feel fearful and defensive, and regard the fleeting pleasures of the world as our only source of satisfaction.

Although all the great religious traditions help us recognize our true Self, the *Course* is unique in emphasizing relationships as the major means for this recognition. As we see and treat others, so do we see and treat ourselves. By recognizing the true Self in others we also find it in ourselves. A "holy relationship" is one that fosters this recognition and extends it in the world.

Remember in your brother you but see yourself.

The Errors of Ego

What is the ego?
But a dream of what you really are.

The ego is the mind's belief
that it is completely on its own.

Who asks you to define the ego
and explain how it arose
can be but he who thinks it real,
and seeks by definition to ensure
that its illusive nature is concealed
behind the words that seem to make it so.

Errors are of the ego,
and correction of errors
lies in the relinquishment of the ego.

Every response to the ego is a call to war,
and war does deprive you of peace.
Yet in this war there is no opponent.

Peace is the ego's greatest enemy because,
according to its interpretation of reality,
war is the guarantee of its survival.
The ego becomes strong in strife.

Even the wished-for can become unwelcome.
That must be so because the ego cannot be at peace.

When you are anxious,
realize that anxiety comes
from the capriciousness of the ego,
and *know this need not be.*
You can be as vigilant against the ego's dictates
as for them.

You Are One Self

You are one Self,
complete and healed and whole,
with power to lift the veil
of darkness from the world.

You are only love, but when you deny this,
you make what you are
something you must learn to remember.

You need to learn to lay all fear aside,
and know your Self as love
which has no opposite in you.

Fear not to look upon the lovely truth in you.

Your Self is still in peace,
even though your mind is in conflict.

Nothing outside yourself can save you;
nothing outside yourself can give you peace.

You will yet learn that peace is part of you,
and requires only that you be there
to embrace any situation in which you are.
And finally you will learn
that there is no limit to where you are,
so that your peace is everywhere,
as you are.

Limit the peace you share,
and your Self must be unknown to you.

What we accept as what we are proclaims
what everyone must be, along with us.
Fail not your brothers, or you fail yourself.
Look lovingly on them, that they may know
that they are part of you, and you of them.

My Self is holy beyond all the thoughts of holiness
of which I now conceive.
Its shimmering and perfect purity
is far more brilliant
than is any light that I have ever looked upon.
Its love is limitless,
with an intensity that holds all things within it,
in the calm of quiet certainty.

Knowing Your Brother

In learning to escape from illusions,
your debt to your brother is something
you must never forget.

Reason sees a holy relationship as what it is;
a common state of mind,
where both give errors gladly to correction,
that both may happily be healed as one.

Whenever you are with a brother,
you are learning what you are
because you are teaching what you are.
He will respond either with pain or with joy,
depending on which teacher you are following.
He will be imprisoned or released
according to your decision,
and so will you.
Never forget your responsibility to him,
because it is your responsibility to yourself.

Look gently on your brother,
and behold the world
in which perception of your hate
has been transformed into a world of love.

We begin the journey back by setting out together,
and gather in our brothers as we continue together.
Every gain in our strength is offered for all,
so they too can lay aside their weakness
and add their strength to us.

How can you find the way
except by taking your brother with you?

Everyone is looking for himself
and for the power and glory he thinks he has lost.
Whenever you are with anyone,
you have another opportunity to find them.

What you acknowledge in your brother
you are acknowledging in yourself,
and what you share you strengthen.

It will be given you to see your brother's worth
when all you want for him is peace.
And what you want for him
you will receive.

Look once again upon your brother,
not without the understanding
that he is the way to Heaven or to hell,
as you perceive him.
But forget not this;
the role you give to him is given you,
and you will walk the way you pointed out to him
because it is your judgment on yourself.

You who are the same
will not decide alone or differently.
Either you give each other life or death;
either you are each other's savior or his judge.

Through your gratitude
you come to know your brother,
and one moment of real recognition
makes everyone your brother.

Know your brother as yourself.
Answer his call for love,
and yours is answered.

To know your brother is to know God.

Each little gift you offer to your brother
lights up the world.

Nothing is asked of you
but to accept the changeless and eternal
that abide in him,
for your Identity is there.
The peace in you can but be found in him.
And every thought of love you offer him
but brings you nearer to your wakening
to peace eternal and to endless joy.

When you have seen your brothers as yourself
you will be released.

The quiet that surrounds you dwells in him,
and from this quiet come the happy dreams
in which your hands are joined in innocence.
These are not hands that grasp in dreams of pain.
They hold no sword,
for they have left their hold
on every vain illusion of this world.
And being empty they receive, instead,
a brother's hand in which completion lies.

This brother neither leads nor follows us,
but walks beside us on the selfsame road.
He is like us,
as near or far away from what we want
as we will let him be.
We make no gains he does not make with us,
and we fall back if he does not advance.
Take not his hand in anger but in love,
for in his progress do you count your own.

Have faith in him who walks with you,
so that your fearful concept of yourself may change.

Choose once again what you would have him be,
remembering that every choice you make
establishes your own identity
as you will see it and believe it is.

When you have become willing to hide nothing,
you will not only be willing
to enter into communion
but will also understand peace and joy.

From the oneness that we have attained
we call to all our brothers,
asking them to share our peace
and consummate our joy.

Let us celebrate our release together
by releasing everyone with us.

Let us unite in bringing blessing to the world.

Our function is to work together,
because apart from each other
we cannot function at all.
The whole power of God's Son
lies in all of us,
but not in any of us alone.

*I would see you as my friend,
that I may remember you are part of me
and come to know myself.*

*Peace to my brother, who is one with me.
Let all the world be blessed with peace through us.*

7

IT IS THROUGH US THAT PEACE WILL COME

The *Course* maintains that we are the essential instruments of peace for the world and that our own thoughts and actions determine how deeply peace is experienced and how widely it is shared. We become the means of peace when we are willing to learn, to teach, to give, and especially to forgive.

The *Course* is distinct among spiritual paths in its emphasis on the importance of forgiveness. Forgiveness of both ourselves and others is said to be crucial for removing fear, anger, and other obstacles that distort our relationships and prevent us from experiencing peace in them.

This world will change through you.
No other means can save it.

To Teach Is to Learn

The only way to have peace is to teach peace.
By teaching peace you must learn it yourself.

In the teaching-learning situation, each one
learns that giving and receiving are the same.
The demarcations they have drawn
between their roles, their minds, their bodies,
their needs, their interests, and all the differences
they thought separated them from one another,
fade and grow dim and disappear.

All good teachers realize
that only fundamental change will last,
but they do not begin at that level.
Strengthening motivation for change
is their first and foremost goal.
It is also their last and final one.
Increasing motivation for change in the learner
is all that a teacher need do to guarantee change.
Change in motivation is a change of mind,
and this will inevitably produce fundamental change
because the mind *is* fundamental.

Your past learning
must have taught you the wrong things,
simply because it has not made you happy.
On this basis alone its value should be questioned.

Understand you but waste time
unless you go beyond what you have learned
to what is yet to learn.

A wise teacher teaches through approach,
not avoidance.
He does not emphasize what you must avoid
to escape from harm,
but what you need to learn to have joy.

Correct and learn, and be open to learning.
You have not made truth,
but truth can still set you free.

To Give Is to Receive

Offer peace to have it yours.

Each gift is an evaluation
of the receiver and the *giver*.

You can give yourself completely,
wholly without loss and only with gain.
Herein lies peace,
for here there *is* no conflict.

Those who offer peace to everyone
have found a home in Heaven
the world cannot destroy.
For it is large enough
to hold the world within its peace.

*Today we will attempt to offer peace to everyone,
and see how quickly peace returns to us.*

I am here only to be truly helpful.

To Let Forgiveness Rest upon All Things

Where could your peace arise
but from forgiveness?

Forgiveness removes only the untrue,
lifting the shadows from the world and carrying it,
safe and sure within its gentleness,
to the bright world of new and clean perception.
There is your purpose *now.*
And it is there that peace awaits you.

Look upon the world with forgiving eyes.
For forgiveness literally transforms vision,
and lets you see the real world
reaching quietly and gently across chaos,
removing all illusions
that had twisted your perception
and fixed it on the past.

To forgive is merely to remember
only the loving thoughts you gave in the past,
and those that were given you.
All the rest must be forgotten.

All that must be forgiven are the illusions
you have held against your brother.

Withhold forgiveness from your brother
and you attack him.
You give him nothing,
and receive of him but what you gave.

Those you do not forgive you fear.

Forgiveness cannot be withheld a little.
Nor is it possible to attack for this and love for that
and understand forgiveness.

Whom you forgive is free,
and what you give you share.
Forgive the sins your brother
thinks he has committed,
and all the guilt you think you see in him.

Forgiveness takes away
what stands between your brother and yourself.
It is the wish that you be joined with him,
and not apart.

Who forgives is healed.
And in his healing lies the proof
that he has truly pardoned,
and retains no trace of condemnation
that he still would hold
against himself or any living thing.

Make way for love, which you did not create,
but which you can extend.
On earth this means forgive your brother,
that the darkness may be lifted from your mind.

How willing are you to forgive your brother?
How much do you desire peace
instead of endless strife and misery and pain?
These questions are the same,
in different form.
Forgiveness is your peace,
for herein lies the end of separation
and the dream of danger and destruction.

If you can see your brother merits pardon,
you have learned forgiveness is your right
as much as his.

You are merely asked to see forgiveness
as the natural reaction
to distress that rests on error,
and thus calls for help.
Forgiveness is the only sane response.

Without forgiveness is the mind in chains,
believing in its own futility.
Yet with forgiveness does the light
shine through the dream of darkness.

The unforgiving mind is full of fear,
and offers love no room to be itself;
no place where it can spread its wings in peace
and soar above the turmoil of the world.
The unforgiving mind is sad,
without the hope of respite and release from pain.
It suffers and abides in misery,
peering about in darkness, seeing not,
yet certain of the danger lurking there.

An unforgiving thought
is one which makes a judgment
that it will not raise to doubt,
although it is not true.
The mind is closed, and will not be released.
The thought protects projection,
tightening its chains,
so that distortions are more veiled
and more obscure; less easily accessible to doubt,
and further kept from reason.

An unforgiving thought does many things.
In frantic action it pursues its goal,
twisting and overturning what it sees
as interfering with its chosen path.
Distortion is its purpose, and the means
by which it would accomplish it as well.
It sets about its furious attempts to smash reality,
without concern for anything that would appear
to pose a contradiction to its point of view.
Forgiveness, on the other hand,
is still, and quietly does nothing.
It offends no aspect of reality,
nor seeks to twist it to appearances it likes.
It merely looks, and waits, and judges not.

There can be no form of suffering
that fails to hide an unforgiving thought.
Nor can there be a form of pain
forgiveness cannot heal.

Forgiveness paints a picture of a world
where suffering is over, loss becomes impossible
and anger makes no sense.
Attack is gone, and madness has an end.

Fear condemns and love forgives.
Forgiveness thus undoes
what fear has produced.

Today we practice true forgiveness,
that the time of joining be no more delayed.

When I have forgiven myself
and remembered who I am,
I will bless everyone and everything I see.

To Bring Peace to the World

This world has much to offer to your peace,
and many chances to extend your own forgiveness.
Such its purpose is,
to those who want to see
peace and forgiveness descend on them,
and offer them the light.

You are entrusted with
the world's release from pain.

The part you play
in salvaging the world from condemnation
is your own escape.

This world awaits the freedom you will give
when you have recognized that you are free.

What cause have you for anger in a world
that merely waits your blessing to be free?

Until forgiveness is complete,
the world does have a purpose.
It becomes the home in which forgiveness is born,
and where it grows and becomes stronger
and more all-embracing.
Here is it nourished, for here it is needed.

We will forgive them all,
absolving all the world
from what we thought it did to us.
For it is we who make the world
as we would have it.

A world in which forgiveness shines on everything,
and peace offers its gentle light to everyone,
is inconceivable to those
who see a world of hatred rising from attack,
poised to avenge, to murder and destroy.
Yet is the world of hatred equally unseen
and inconceivable to those
who feel God's love in them.
Their world reflects the quietness and peace
that shines in them;
the gentleness and innocence
they see surrounding them;
the joy with which they look out
from the endless wells of joy within.
What they have felt in them they look upon,
and see its sure reflection everywhere.

What would you see?
The choice is given you.
But learn and do not let your mind forget
this law of seeing:
You will look upon that which you feel within.
If hatred finds a place within your heart,
you will perceive a fearful world,
held cruelly in death's sharp-pointed, bony fingers.
If you feel the Love of God within you,
you will look out on a world of mercy and of love.

If you choose to see a world without an enemy,
in which you are not helpless,
the means to see it will be given you.

No longer is the world our enemy,
for we have chosen that we be its Friend.

My forgiveness is the means
by which the world is healed,
together with myself.
Let me then, forgive the world,
that it may be healed along with me.

8

The Gifts of Peace

When peace is welcomed, it brings with it many gifts, among them healing, freedom, and love. Like peace, these gifts cannot be kept for ourselves alone but rather must be shared with others if we are to know them as our own.

> *You understand that you are healed*
> *when you give healing.*
> *You accept forgiveness as accomplished in yourself*
> *when you forgive.*
> *You recognize your brother as yourself,*
> *and thus do you perceive that you are whole.*

Healing

Peace must come to those who choose to heal
and not to judge.

The decision to heal and to be healed
is the first step toward recognizing
what you truly want.
Every attack is a step away from this,
and every healing thought brings it closer.

Healing will flash across your open mind,
as peace and truth arise
to take the place of war and vain imaginings.

Healing is release from the fear of waking
and the substitution of the decision to wake.
The decision to wake
is the reflection of the will to love,
since all healing involves replacing fear with love.

Would you not prefer to heal
what has been broken,
and join in making whole
what has been ravaged by separation and disease?
You have been called,
together with your brother,
to the most holy function this world contains.
It is the only one that has no limits,
and reaches out to every broken
fragment of the Sonship
with healing and uniting comfort.

You will be made whole
As you make whole.

No one can ask another to be healed.
But he can let *himself* be healed,
and thus offer the other what he has received.
Who can bestow upon another
what he does not have?
And who can share what he denies himself?

Those whom you heal bear witness to your healing,
for in their wholeness you will see your own.

We will try today to find the source of healing,
which is in our minds. . . .
It is not farther from us than ourselves.
It is as near to us as our own thoughts;
so close it is impossible to lose.
We need but seek it, and it must be found.

Our function is to let our minds be healed,
that we may carry healing to the world,
exchanging curse for blessing, pain for joy,
and separation for the peace of God.

*Peace fills my heart,
and floods my body
with the purpose of forgiveness.
Now my mind is healed.*

Freedom

Who could be set free
while he imprisons anyone?
A jailer is not free,
for he is bound together with his prisoner.

Look about the world,
and see the suffering there.
Is not your heart willing
to bring your weary brothers rest?
They must await your own release.
They stay in chains till you are free.
They cannot see the mercy of the world
until you find it in yourself.

In your freedom lies the freedom of the world.

You can escape all bondage of the world,
and give the world the same release you found.
You can remember what the world forgot,
and offer it your own remembering.

As we offer freedom,
it is given us.

Love

In honesty, is it not harder for you to say
"I love" than "I hate"?
You associate love with weakness
and hatred with strength,
and your own real power seems to you
as your real weakness.
For you could not control
your joyous response to the call of love
if you heard it.

By not offering total love
you will not be healed completely.

Love always answers,
being unable to deny a call for help,
or not to hear the cries of pain that rise to it
from every part of this strange world.

The opposite of love is fear,
but what is all encompassing
can have no opposite.

Perfect love casts out fear.
If fear exists,
Then there is not perfect love.

Whenever you are not wholly joyous,
it is because you have reacted with a lack of love.

You have so little faith in yourself
because you are unwilling to accept the fact
that perfect love is in you.
And so you seek without
for what you cannot find without.

Everyone seeks for love as you do,
but knows it not unless he joins with you
in seeking it.

The attraction of love for love
remains irresistible.
For it is the function of love
to unite all things unto itself,
and to hold all things together
by extending its wholeness.

As you release, so will you be released.
Forget this not,
or love will be unable
to find you and comfort you.

Love's arms are open to receive you,
and give you peace forever.

Love wishes to be known,
completely understood and shared.
It has no secrets;
nothing that it would keep apart and hide.

Love does not seek for power,
but for relationships.

Truth does not struggle against ignorance,
and love does not attack fear.

Love can have no enemy.

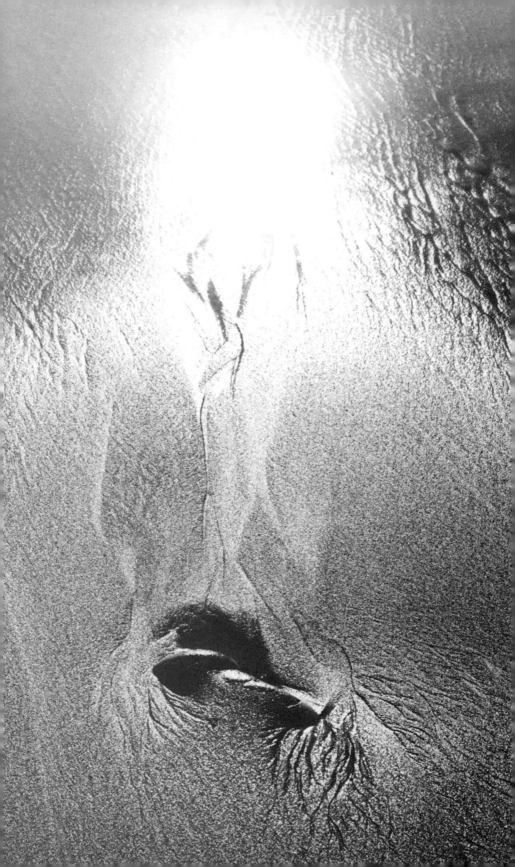

Be not afraid of love.
For it alone can heal all sorrow.

Fail not in your function
of loving in a loveless place
made out of darkness and deceit,
for thus are darkness and deceit undone.

The holiest of all the spots on earth
is where an ancient hatred
has become a present love.

Love cannot be far behind
a grateful heart and thankful mind.

There is no room in us for fear today,
for we have welcomed love into our hearts.

We are deceived no longer.
Love has now returned to our awareness.
And we are at peace again,
for fear has gone and only love remains.

Love holds no grievances.
When I let all my grievances go
I will know I am perfectly safe.

9

THE WAY TO PEACE IS OPEN

The way to peace is open, but each of us must choose whether or not to follow it. The *Course* suggests, however, that our final choice is certain, since peace is truly our deepest desire and the only alternative is to languish in dreams of pain and conflict. We can delay, but why would we want to, when on our choice rests the welfare and peace of the world and when peace is freely available for all.

Make way for peace
and it will come.

The Way to Peace Is Open

There is a silence
into which the world cannot intrude.
There is an ancient peace
you carry in your heart
and have not lost.

Peace is a natural heritage of spirit.
Everyone is free to refuse to accept his inheritance,
but he is not free to establish
what his inheritance is.

Peace and understanding go together
and never can be found alone.

Strength and innocence are not in conflict,
but naturally live in peace.

Lay down your arms,
and come without defense into the quiet place
where Heaven's peace holds all things still at last.
Lay down all thoughts of danger and of fear.
Let no attack enter with you.

In this quiet state alone
is strength and power.
Here can no weakness enter,
for here is no attack
and therefore no illusions.

Peace is of God.
You who are part of God
are not at home except in His peace.

Abide in peace,
where God would have you be.

God knows you only in peace,
and this is your reality.

His peace surrounds you silently.
God is very quiet.

Look with peace upon your brothers,
and God will come rushing into your heart
in gratitude for your gift to Him.

The peace of God passeth your understanding
only in the past.
Yet here it *is,*
and you can understand it *now.*

"I want the peace of God."
To say these words is nothing.
But to mean these words is everything. . . .
No one can mean these words and not be healed.
He cannot play with dreams,
nor think he is himself a dream.
He cannot make a hell and think it real.
He wants the peace of God,
and it is given him.
For that is all he wants,
and that is all he will receive.
Many have said these words.
But few indeed have meant them.
You have but to look upon
the world you see around you
to be sure how very few they are.

We want the peace of God.
This is no idle wish.
These words do not request
another dream be given us.
They do not ask for compromise,
nor try to make another bargain in the hope
that there may yet be one that can succeed
where all the rest have failed.
To mean these words acknowledges
illusions are in vain,
requesting the eternal in the place of shifting dreams
which seem to change in what they offer,
but are one in nothingness.

"There is no peace except the peace of God."
Seek you no further.
You will not find peace
except the peace of God.
Accept this fact,
and save yourself the agony
of yet more bitter disappointments, bleak despair,
and sense of icy hopelessness and doubt.
Seek you no further.
There is nothing else for you to find
except the peace of God.

A Gift of Healing

1

THE DESIRE FOR
HEALING

The health of our bodies and the state of our world reflect our desires and defenses, fantasies and fears. If we would be healed we must relinquish these unhealthly motives and replace them with the desire for healing. We must also relinquish mental habits—such as anger, attack, and the sense of individual specialness—that separate us from others. Indeed, this sense of separation *is* our sickness.

The *Course* emphasizes that healing cannot be for ourselves alone, for in reality we are not alone and separate. We must help each other, and thus relationships become a central focus for healing. The *Course* says, "In your brother you but see yourself." Our desire to find a better way therefore becomes a driving force for healing both ourselves and others.

As we ourselves are healed, we provide an example for others. And as we desire to help and heal others, we ourselves are also healed. The result is that relationships become "a temple of healing" in which healing is recognized as a collaborative venture that leads to the recognition of our underlying unity.

Your function in this world is healing.

The Decision to Heal

The decision to heal and to be healed
is the first step toward recognizing
what you truly want.
Every attack is a step away from this,
and every healing thought
brings it closer.

To be healed is to pursue one goal,
because you have accepted only one
and want but one.

Nothing is harmful or beneficent
apart from what you wish.
It is your wish
that makes it what it is
in its effects on you.

There is no miracle
you cannot have
when you desire healing.
But there is no miracle
that can be given you
unless you want it.

Your function on earth is healing. . . .
As long as you believe you have other functions,
so long will you need correction.
For this belief is the destruction of peace.

Healing will always stand aside
when it would be seen as threat.
The instant it is welcome it is there.
Where healing has been given
it will be received.

You have been called,
together with your brother,
to the most holy function
this world contains.
It is the only one
that has no limits,
and reaches out
to every broken fragment of the Sonship
with healing and uniting comfort.
This is offered you,
in your holy relationship.
Accept it here,
and you will give
as you have accepted.

Suffice it, then, that you have work to do
to play your part.
The ending must remain obscure to you
until your part is done.
It does not matter.
For your part is still
what all the rest depends on.

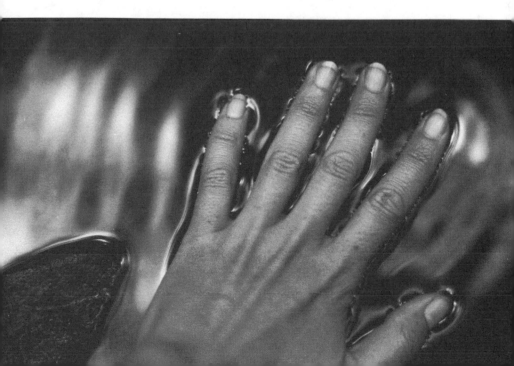

The Conditions of Healing

Healing is the effect of minds that join,
as sickness comes from minds that separate.

If you are unwilling
to perceive an appeal for help
as what it is,
it is because you are unwilling
to give help and receive it.
To fail to recognize a call for help
is to refuse to help.
Would you maintain that you do not need it?
Yet this is what you are maintaining
when you refuse to recognize a brother's appeal,
for only by answering his appeal
can you be helped.

Your interpretations of your brother's needs
are your interpretations of yours.
By giving help you are asking for it.

It may help someone to point out
where he is heading,
but the point is lost
unless he is also helped
to change his direction.
The unhealed healer cannot do this for him,
since he cannot do it for himself.
The only meaningful contribution
the healer can make
is to present an example
of one whose direction
has been changed for him,
and who no longer believes
in nightmares of any kind.

Healing perceives nothing in the healer
that everyone else does not share with him.

Healing sees no specialness at all.
It does not come from pity
but from love.

There is no sadness
where a miracle has come to heal.
And nothing more than just one instant
of your love without attack is necessary
that all this occur.
In that one instant you are healed,
and in that single instant
is all healing done.

Healing reflects our joint will.
This is obvious when you consider
what healing is for.
Healing is the way in which
the separation is overcome.

You have learned your need of healing.
Would you bring anything else to the Sonship,
recognizing your need of healing for yourself?

Accept the miracle of healing,
and it will go forth
because of what it is.
It is its nature to extend itself
the instant it is born.
And it is born
the instant it is offered and received.

No one can ask another to be healed.
But he can let himself be healed,
and thus offer the other
what he has received.
Who can bestow upon another
what he does not have?
And who can share
what he denies himself?

If you wish only to be healed,
you heal.
Your single purpose makes this possible.
But if you are afraid of healing,
then it cannot come through you.
The only thing that is required for a healing
is lack of fear.
The fearful are not healed,
and cannot heal.
This does not mean the conflict
must be gone forever from your mind to heal.
For if it were,
there were no need for healing then.
But it does mean, if only for an instant,
you love without attack.
An instant is sufficient.
Miracles wait not on time.

The only way to heal
is to be healed.

Those who are healed
become the instruments
of healing.

Healing One Another

Healing is a collaborative venture.

It is impossible that anyone be healed alone.
In sickness must he be apart and separate.
But healing is his own decision to be one again,
and to accept his Self.

Fail not your brothers, or you fail yourself.
Look lovingly on them, that they may know
that they are part of you, and you of them.

From you can come their rest.
From you can rise a world
they will rejoice to look upon,
and where their hearts are glad.
In you there is a vision
that extends to all of them,
and covers them in gentleness and light.

Perhaps you will not recognize them all,
nor realize how great your offering
to all the world,
when you let healing come to you.

Let yourself be healed
that you may be forgiving,
offering salvation to your brother
and yourself.

Your healing saves him pain
as well as you,
and you are healed
because you wished him well.

Your healing is the witness unto his,
and cannot be apart from his at all.

Spend but an instant in the glad acceptance
of what is given you to give your brother,
and learn with him
what has been given both of you.

And you will understand
his safety is your own,
and in his healing you are healed.

When a brother behaves insanely,
you can heal him
only by perceiving the sanity in him.

It is given you to show him, by your healing
that his guilt is but the fabric
of a senseless dream.

You have reached the end of an ancient journey,
not realizing yet that it is over.
You are still worn and tired,
and the desert's dust still seems
to cloud your eyes and keep you sightless.
Yet He Whom you welcomed has come to you,
and would welcome you.
He has waited long to give you this.
Receive it now of Him,
for He would have you know Him.
Only a little wall of dust
still stands between you.
Blow on it lightly and with happy laughter,
and it will fall away.
And walk into the garden
love has prepared for both of you.

Look upon your brother as yourself.
Your relationship is now a temple of healing;
a place where all the weary ones
can come and rest.

Use no relationship
to hold you to the past,
but with each one each day
be born again.
A minute, even less,
will be enough
to free you from the past.

Let us together follow in the way
that truth points out to us.
And let us be the leaders of our many brothers
who are seeking for the way, but find it not.

We go beyond the veil of fear,
lighting each other's way.
The holiness that leads us
is within us, as is our home.

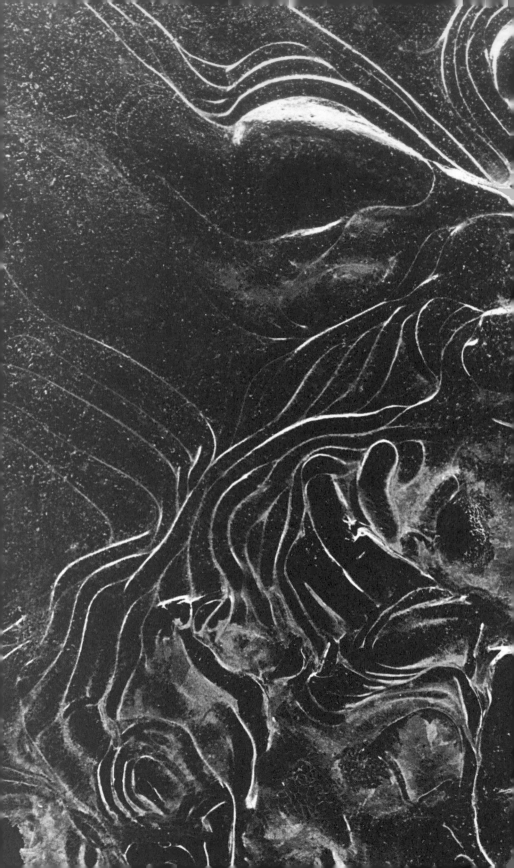

2

THE DREAM OF
SICKNESS

In our collective dream we take ourselves to be bodies, separate from God and from each other. The limits of the body, its sickness, suffering, and death, seem terrifyingly real and inescapable. We seem to be helpless victims of the body and world, able to enjoy fleeting pleasures for only a moment before they are snatched away again. Small wonder, then, that we live in so much fear.

This fear, says the *Course,* is both cause and effect of our dreams. It is an illusion based not on present reality, but on an imagined future. Like all illusions it is self-masking, hiding its unreality in the distortions of perception it induces. Only by looking carefully at all illusions can their distortions, unreality and lack of power over us be recognized. To look carefully at our fears and illusions is therefore to see through them. Once we see clearly, separation is recognized as "merely a faulty formulation of reality, with no effect at all." The body is seen as merely a symbol of what we thought we were, and the true function of both the world and the body is recognized as healing.

> *Forgiveness is the great need of this world*
> *but that is because it is a world of illusions.*

The Veil of Illusion

What is healing but the removal
of all that stands in the way of knowledge?
And how else can one dispel illusions
except by looking at them directly,
without protecting them?
Be not afraid, therefore,
for what you will be looking at
is the source of fear,
and you are beginning to learn
that fear is not real.

All illusions are of fear,
and they can be of nothing else.

No illusions can attract
the mind that has transcended them,
and left them far behind.

How easily do idols go
when they are still perceived
but wanted not.
How willingly the mind
can let them go
when it has understood
that idols are nothing and nowhere,
and are purposeless.

Forget not, then, that idols
must keep hidden what you are,
not from the Mind of God
but from your own.

There can be no order of difficulty in healing
merely because all sickness is illusion.

Be you thankful
that there is a place
where truth and beauty wait for you.
Go on to meet them gladly,
and learn how much awaits you
for the simple willingness
to give up nothing
because it is nothing.

There is no gap that separates
the truth from dreams
and from illusions.
Truth has left no room for them
in any place or time.
For it fills every place
and every time.

Separation Is Sickness

The world you perceive
is a world of separation.

The separation is merely
a faulty formulation of reality,
with no effect at all.

Separation is no more
than an illusion of despair.

Replace your dream of separation
with the fact of unity.
For the separation is only
the denial of union,
and correctly interpreted
attests to your eternal knowledge
that union is true.

A sick person perceives himself
as separate from God.
Would you see him as separate from you?
It is your task to heal the sense of separation
that has made him sick.
It is your function to recognize for him
that what he believes about himself
is not the truth.
It is your forgiveness
that must show him this.
Healing is very simple.

Sickness is not of the body,
but of the mind.

The acceptance of sickness
as a decision of the mind,
for a purpose for which it would use the body,
is the basis of healing.
And this is so for healing in all forms.
A patient decides that this is so,
and he recovers.
If he decides against recovery,
he will not be healed.
Who is the physician?
Only the mind of the patient himself.
The outcome is what he decides that it is.

Healing involves an understanding
of what the illusion of sickness is for.
Healing is impossible without this.

You are afraid to know God's Will,
because you believe it is not yours.
This belief is your whole sickness
and your whole fear.
Every symptom of sickness and fear
arises here,
because this is the belief
that makes you *want* not to know.
Believing this you hide in darkness,
denying that the light is in you.

The acceptance of peace
is the denial of illusion,
and sickness is an illusion.

We attend in silence and in joy.
This is the day when healing comes to us.
This is the day when separation ends,
and we remember Who we really are.

Limitations of the Body

The body is the symbol
of what you think you are.

You have made of it a symbol
for the limitations
that you want your mind
to have and see and keep.

If you use the body for attack,
it is harmful to you.
If you use it only to reach the minds
of those who believe they are bodies,
and teach them through the body
this is not so, you will understand
the power of the mind that is in you.

Sickness is anger taken out upon the body,
so that it will suffer pain.

You are not sick
and you cannot die.
But you can confuse yourself
with things that do.

"I am not a body. I am free."
It is essential for your progress in this course
that you accept today's idea,
and hold it very dear.
Be not concerned that to the ego
it is quite insane.
The ego holds the body dear
because it dwells in it,
and lives united with the home that it has made.
It is part of the illusion that has sheltered it
from being found illusory itself.

The ego uses the body for attack,
for pleasure and for pride.
The insanity of this perception
makes it a fearful one indeed.
The Holy Spirit sees the body only
as a means of communication,
and because communicating is sharing
it becomes communion.

Regard bodies solely
as a means of joining minds
and uniting them with yours and mine.
This interpretation of the body
will change your mind entirely about its value.

In the service of uniting
it becomes a beautiful lesson
in communion, which has value
until communion is.

Healing is the result of using the body
solely for communication.

To see a body as anything
except a means of communication
is to limit your mind and to hurt yourself.

You are not limited by the body. . . .
Yet mind can be manifested
through the body if it goes beyond it
and does not interpret it as limitation.
Whenever you see another
as limited to or by the body,
you are imposing this limit on yourself.
Are you willing to accept this,
when your whole purpose for learning
should be to escape from limitations?

Use it for truth and you will see it truly.
Misuse it and you will misunderstand it.

Health is the result of relinquishing
all attempts to use the body lovelessly.

Help and healing are the normal expressions
of a mind that is working through the body,
but not in it.

The mind can heal the body,
but the body cannot heal the mind.

When the body ceases to attract you,
and when you place no value on it
as a meaning of getting anything,
then there will be no interference in communication
and your thoughts will be as free as God's.

"I am not a body, I am free.
For I am still as God created me."

The World You See

This is an insane world,
and do not underestimate
the extent of its insanity.
There is no area of your perception
that it has not touched.

Learn to look upon the world
as a means of healing the separation.

Be healed that you may heal.

Your healing will extend,
and will be brought to problems
that you thought were not your own.

Healing replaces suffering.
Who looks on one cannot perceive the other,
for they cannot both be there.
And what you see the world will witness,
and will witness to.
Thus is your healing
everything the world requires,
that it may be healed.

You do not want the world.
The only thing of value in it
is whatever part of it
you look upon with love.
This gives it the only reality it will ever have.

The resurrection of the world
awaits your healing
and your happiness.

The world becomes a place of hope,
because its only purpose is to be a place
where hope of happiness can be fulfilled.
And no one stands outside this hope . . .
the purpose of the world
is one which all must share,
if hope be more than just a dream.

Come to the holy instant and be healed,
for nothing that is there received
is left behind on your returning to the world.
And being blessed you will bring blessing.
Life is given you to give the dying world.

When I am healed I am not healed alone.
And I would share my healing with the world,
that sickness may be banished from the mind
of God's one Son, who is my only Self.

Today I choose to see a world forgiven.

Time and Eternity

Healing in time is needed,
for joy cannot establish
its eternal reign
where sorrow dwells.

Accept only the function of healing in time,
because that is what time is for.

If you accept your function
in the world of time as one of healing,
you will emphasize only the aspect of time
in which healing can occur.
Healing cannot be accomplished in the past.
It must be accomplished in the present
to release the future.
This interpretation ties the future to the present,
and extends the present rather than the past.

Old ideas about time are very difficult to change,
because everything you believe is rooted in time,
and depends on your not learning
these new ideas about it.
Yet that is precisely why
you need new ideas about time.

All of time
is but the mad belief
that what is over
is still here and now.

The one wholly true thought
one can hold about the past
is that it is not here.
To think about it at all
is therefore to think about illusions.

All healing is release from the past.

There is no fantasy that does not contain
the dream of retribution for the past.
Would you act out the dream,
or let it go?

Everyone seen without the past
thus brings you nearer to the end of time
by bringing healed and healing sight
into the darkness,
and enabling the world to see.

Delay does not matter in eternity,
but it is tragic in time.
You have elected to be in time
rather than eternity, and therefore
believe you are in time.

While time lasts in your mind
there will be choices.
Time itself is your choice.
If you would remember eternity
you must look only on the eternal.
Time and eternity cannot both be real,
because they contradict each other.
If you will accept
only what is timeless as real,
you will begin to understand eternity
and make it yours.

The reflections you accept
into the mirror of your mind in time
but bring eternity nearer or farther.
But eternity itself is beyond all time.
Reach out of time and touch it,
with the help of its reflection in you.

Delay will hurt you now more than before,
only because you realize it is delay,
and that escape from pain is really possible.

If you are tempted to be dispirited
by thinking how long it would take
to change your mind so completely,
ask yourself, "How long is an instant?"

How long is an instant?
As long as it takes to reestablish
perfect sanity, perfect peace
and perfect love for everyone.

The working out of all correction
takes no time at all.
Yet the acceptance of the working out
can seem to take forever.

Now is the release from time.

The only interval in which
I can be saved from time is now.
For in this instant has forgiveness come
to set me free.

Future loss is not your fear.
But present joining is your dread.
Who can feel desolation except now?
A future cause as yet has no effects.
And therefore must it be that if you fear,
there is a present cause.
And it is this that needs correction,
not a future state.

You are but asked to let the future go,
and place it in God's Hands.
And you will see by your experience
that you have laid the past and present
in His Hands as well,
because the past will punish you no more,
and future dread will now be meaningless.
Release the future.
For the past is gone,
and what is present,
freed from its bequest
of grief and misery,
of pain and loss,
becomes the instant in which time
escapes the bondage of illusions
where it runs its pitiless, inevitable course.
Then is each instant which was slave to time
transformed into a holy instant,
when the light that was kept hidden in God's Son
is freed to bless the world.
Now is he free, and all his glory
shines upon a world made free with him,
to share his holiness.

Place, then, your future in the Hands of God.
For thus you call the memory of Him to come again,
replacing all your thoughts of sin and evil
with the truth of love.
Think you the world could fail to gain thereby,
and every living creature not respond
with healed perception?
Who entrusts himself to God
has also placed the world within the Hands
to which he has himself appealed
for comfort and security.
He lays aside the sick illusions of the world
along with his
and offers peace to both.

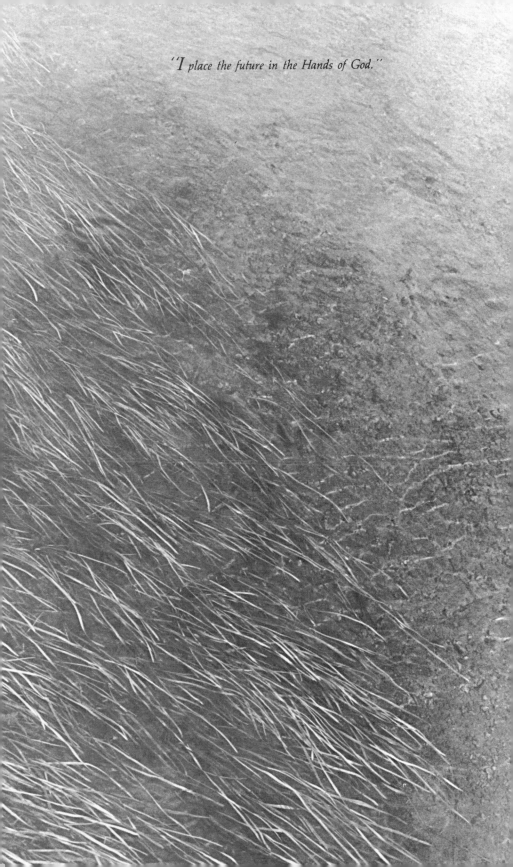

"*I place the future in the Hands of God.*"

From Fear to Faith

Healing is a way of forgetting
the sense of danger
the ego has induced in you,
by not recognizing its existence
in your brother.

Fear is a symptom
of your own deep sense of loss.
If when you perceive it in others
you learn to supply the loss,
the basic cause of fear is removed.
Thereby you teach yourself
that fear does not exist in you.
The means for removing it is in yourself
and you have demonstrated this by giving it.

Fear cannot long be hidden by illusions,
for it is part of them.
It will escape and take another form,
being the source of all illusions.

You must remember, however,
that the *Course* states, and repeatedly,
that its purpose is the escape from fear.

You too will laugh at your fears
and replace them with peace.
For fear lies not in reality,
but in the minds of children
who do not understand reality.
It is only their lack of understanding
that frightens them,
and when they learn to perceive truly
they are not afraid.

The more you look at fear the less you see it,
and the clearer what it conceals becomes.

Very simply, then,
you may believe you are afraid of nothingness,
but you are really afraid of nothing.
And in that awareness you are healed.

The "fearful healer"
is a contradiction in terms.

An individual may ask for physical healing
because he is fearful of bodily harm.
At the same time,
if he were healed physically,
the threat to his thought system
might be considerably more fearful to him
than its physical expression.
In this case he is not really asking
for release from fear,
but for the removal of a symptom
that he himself selected.
This request is, therefore, not for healing at all.

Fear does not gladden.
Healing does.
Fear always makes exceptions.
Healing never does.
Fear produces dissociation,
because it induces separation.
Healing always produces harmony,
because it proceeds from integration.

Give faith to one another
for faith and hope and mercy
are yours to give.
Into the hands that give, the gift is given.

By faith, you offer the gift
of freedom from the past.

Realize that there is nothing
faith cannot forgive.
No error interferes
with its calm sight.

To have faith is to heal.

All fear is past
because its source is gone,
and all its thoughts gone with it.
Love remains the only present state.

3

THE CAUSES OF
THE DREAM

Our dream, says the *Course*, is a dream of attack and vengeance. We attack ourselves and one another for our imagined sins, while in reality our Self remains untouched by such illusions. Yet because we take the dream to be reality, its effects seem equally real. Our imagined attacks create fear, guilt, and anger, which seem to justify further attack. Thus a vicious cycle is set up and the dream is perpetuated.

Only by changing our minds, the source of both the cause and cure of the dream, can we hope to awaken. This requires that we learn to shift our perception from a focus on mistakes, our own and those of others, to a focus on the underlying love and innocence that are our true nature. To the extent that we do this, we will realize that anger, attack, and guilt are unjustified, and our dream of vengeance will be recognized for the illusion that it is.

You are the dreamer
of the world of dreams.

Attack and Blame

There is nothing to prevent you
from recognizing all calls for help
as exactly what they are,
except your own imagined
need to attack.
It is only this
that makes you willing to engage
in endless "battles" with reality
in which you deny the reality
of the need for healing
by making it unreal.
You would not do this
except for your unwillingness
to accept reality as it is.

It is when judgment ceases
that healing occurs.

We are restored to sanity,
in which we understand
that anger is insane, attack is mad,
and vengeance merely foolish fantasy.

The response of holiness
to any form of error
is always the same.
There is no contradiction
in what holiness calls forth.
Its one response is healing.

As blame is withdrawn from without,
there is a strong tendency
to harbor it within.
It is difficult at first to realize
that this is exactly the same thing,
for there is no distinction
between within and without.

If your brothers are part of you
and you blame them for your deprivation,
you are blaming yourself.
And you cannot blame yourself
without blaming them.
That is why blame must be undone,
not seen elsewhere.
Lay it to yourself
and you cannot know yourself,
for only the ego blames at all.
Self-blame is therefore ego identification,
and as much an ego defense
as blaming others.

Come wholly without condemnation,
for otherwise you will believe
that the door is barred
and you cannot enter.
The door is not barred,
and it is impossible that you cannot enter
the place where God would have you be.

Escape from Guilt

Relieve the mind
of the insane burden of guilt
it carries so wearily,
and healing is accomplished.

You are whole only in your guiltlessness,
and only in your guiltlessness
can you be happy.

Guiltlessness is invulnerability.

As long as you feel guilty
you are listening to the voice of the ego.

When you maintain that you are guilty
but the source of your guilt lies in the past,
you are not looking inward.
The past is not in you.
Your weird associations to it
have no meaning in the present.
Yet you let them stand
between you and your brothers,
with whom you find
no real relationships at all.

No real relationship can rest on guilt.

Who is there but wishes to be free of pain?
He may not yet have learned
how to exchange guilt for innocence,
nor realize that only in this exchange
can freedom from pain be his.
Yet those who have failed to learn
need teaching, not attack.

The end of guilt
is in your hands to give.
Would you stop now
to look for guilt in one another?

You restore guiltlessness
to whomever you see as guiltless.

From everyone whom you accord
release from guilt
you will inevitably learn your innocence.

In the crystal cleanness
of the release you give
is your instantaneous escape from guilt.

All salvation is escape from guilt.

The Power of Perception

Do you not see that all your misery
comes from the strange belief
that you are powerless?

Uncorrected error of any kind
deceives you about the power
that is in you to make correction.

You see what you expect,
and you expect what you invite.
Your perception is the result of your invitation,
coming to you as you sent for it.

The value of deciding in advance
what you want to happen
is simply that you will perceive the situation
as a means to make it happen.
You will therefore make every effort
to overlook what interferes
with the accomplishment of your objective.

Perception has a focus.
It is this that gives consistency
to what you see.
Change but this focus,
and what you behold will change accordingly.
Your vision now will shift,
to give support to the intent
which has replaced the one you held before.

It is still up to you
to choose to join with truth
or with illusion.
But remember that to choose one
is to let the other go.
Which one you choose
you will endow with beauty and reality,
because the choice depends
on which you value more.
The spark of beauty
or the veil of ugliness,
the real world
or the world of guilt and fear,
truth or illusion,
freedom or slavery.

The power to heal the Son of God is given you
because he must be one with you.
You are responsible for how he sees himself.
And reason tells you it is given you
to change his whole mind,
which is one with you,
in just an instant.
And any instant serves
to bring complete correction of his errors
and make him whole.
The instant that you choose
to let yourself be healed,
in that same instant is his whole salvation
seen as complete with yours.

The miracle is a lesson
in total perception.

To heal, then, is to correct perception
in your brother and yourself.

The reestablishing of meaning
in a chaotic thought system
is the way to heal it.

It is but your thoughts
that bring you fear,
and your deliverance
depends on you.

What I see reflects a process in my mind,
which starts with my idea of what I want.

I can be hurt
by nothing but my thoughts.

We practice coming nearer
to the light in us today.
We take our wandering thoughts,
and gently bring them back
to where they fall in line
with all the thoughts we share with God.
We will not let them stray.
We let the light within our minds
direct them to come home.

I can elect to change
all thoughts that hurt.
And I would go beyond these words today,
and past all reservations,
and arrive at full acceptance
of the truth in them.

Learning and Teaching

The essential thing is learning
that you do not know.

Those who remember always
that they know nothing,
and who have become willing
to learn everything, will learn it.

Trials are but lessons
that you failed to learn
presented once again,
so where you made a faulty choice before
you now can make a better one,
and thus escape all pain
that what you chose before has brought to you.

Healing thus becomes
a lesson in understanding,
and the more you practice it
the better teacher and learner you become.

You can learn to bless,
and cannot give what you have not.
If, then, you offer blessing,
it must have come first to yourself.
And you must also have accepted it as yours,
for how else could you give it away?

If you have denied truth,
what better witnesses
to its reality could you have
than those who have been healed by it?
But be sure to count yourself among them,
for in your willingness to join them
is your healing accomplished.

All things are lessons
God would have me learn.

Today I learn to give
as I receive.

What you made has imprisoned your will,
and given you a sick mind
that must be healed.
Your vigilance against this sickness
is the way to heal it.
Once your mind is healed it radiates health,
and thereby teaches healing.
This establishes you as a teacher.

Teaching is done in many ways,
above all by example.
Teaching should be healing,
because it is the sharing
of ideas.

When a teacher of God fails to heal,
it is because he has forgotten Who he is.

In order to heal,
it thus becomes essential
for the teacher of God
to let all his own mistakes be corrected.

Teach only love,
for that is what you are.

A Change of Mind

Anyone is free to change his mind,
and all his thoughts change with it.
Now the source of thought has shifted,
for to change your mind
means you have changed the source
of all ideas you think or ever thought
or yet will think.
You free the past from what you thought before.
You free the future from all ancient thoughts
of seeking what you do not want to find.

There can be nothing
that a change of mind cannot affect,
for all external things are only shadows
of a decision already made.
Change the decision,
and how can its shadow be unchanged?

Sickness is of the mind,
and has nothing to do with the body.
What does this recognition "cost"?
It costs the whole world you see,
for the world will never again
appear to rule the mind.
For with this recognition
is responsibility placed where it belongs;
not with the world,
but on him who looks on the world
and sees it as it is not.
He looks on what he chooses to see.
No more and no less.
The world does nothing to him.
He only thought it did.
Nor does he do anything to the world,
because he was mistaken about what it is.
Herein is the release
from guilt and sickness both,
for they are one.

Knowledge cannot dawn on a mind
full of illusions,
because truth and illusions
are irreconcilable.
Truth is whole,
and cannot be known
by part of a mind.

All forms of sickness
are signs that the mind is split,
and does not accept
a unified purpose.

When you limit yourself
we are not of one mind,
and that is sickness.

The miracle comes quietly
into the mind that stops an instant and is still.
It reaches gently from that quiet time,
and from the mind it healed in quiet then,
to other minds to share its quietness.
And they will join in doing nothing
to prevent its radiant extension
back into the Mind Which caused all minds to be.
Born out of sharing,
there can be no pause in time
to cause the miracle delay
in hastening to all unquiet minds,
and bringing them an instant's stillness,
when the memory of God returns to them.

The power of one mind
can shine into another,
because all the lamps of God
were lit by the same spark.
It is everywhere
and it is eternal.

Your mind is so powerful a light
that you can look into theirs
and enlighten them,
as I can enlighten yours.
I want to share my mind with you
because we are of one Mind,
and that Mind is ours.
See only this Mind everywhere,
because only this is everywhere
and in everything.
It is everything
because it encompasses
all things within itself.
Blessed are you who perceive only this,
because you perceive only what is true.

When a mind has only light,
it knows only light.
Its own radiance shines all around it,
and extends out into the darkness
of other minds,
transforming them into majesty.

The mind that is made willing
to accept God's gifts
has been restored to spirit,
and extends its freedom and its joy.

4

THE MEANS OF
AWAKENING

To awaken from our dream of pain and suffering, we must first recognize that we are dreaming. Only then will we see that dreaming is our choice, that we can create dreams of happiness instead of pain, and that we can ultimately awaken from all dreams. Because the dreams of this world are so filled with fear, the *Course* says that it is very difficult for us to view even reality and awakening without fear. Therefore, instead of hurling us abruptly into reality while we still dread it, the *Course* offers a gentle progressive change of mind in which our dreams of fear are changed to dreams of happiness, our dreams of anger and attack to dreams of gratitude and forgiveness.

These happy dreams reflect reality and our natural state, which are loving and joyous. This shift in perception from fear to love is what is called a *miracle.* It shows us that we are the creators of our dreams and it points beyond all dreams to awakening.

The *Course* focuses on healing relationships as a means of mutual awakening. These relationships may occur spontaneously, but sometimes a formal psychotherapeutic relationship can also be helpful. Relationship is central to the healing process and whether in therapy or not, we are both patient and therapist, student and teacher for each other.

Healing is release from the fear of waking
and the substitution of the decision to wake.

Awakening from the Dream

The dreamer of a dream is not awake,
but does not know he sleeps.
He sees illusions of himself
as sick or well, depressed or happy.

What is done in dreams
has not really been done.
It is impossible to convince
the dreamer that this is so,
for dreams are what they are
because of their illusion of reality.
Only in waking is the full release from them,
for only then does it become perfectly apparent
that they had no effect upon reality at all,
and did not change it.

Yet if you are the dreamer,
you perceive this much at least:
That you have caused the dream,
and can accept another dream as well.
But for this change in content in the dream,
it must be realized that it is you
who dreamed the dreaming that you do not like.
It is but an effect that you have caused.

Nothing at all has happened
but that you have put yourself to sleep,
and dreamed a dream
in which you were alien to yourself,
and but a part of someone else's dream.
The miracle does not awaken you,
but merely shows you who the dreamer is.
It teaches you there is a choice of dreams
while you are still asleep,
depending on the purpose of your dreaming.
Do you wish for dreams of healing,
or for dreams of death?

A dream is like a memory
in that it pictures
what you wanted shown to you.

The dreams forgiveness lets the mind perceive
do not induce another form of sleep,
so that the dreamer dreams another dream.
His happy dreams are heralds of the dawn
of truth upon the mind.
They lead from sleep to gentle waking,
so that dreams are gone.

In forgiving dreams is no one asked
to be the victim and the sufferer.
These are the happy dreams.

This world is full of miracles.
They stand in shining silence
next to every dream of pain and suffering,
of sin and guilt.
They are the dream's alternative,
the choice to be the dreamer,
rather than deny the active role
in making up the dream.

When you accept a miracle,
you do not add your dream of fear
to one that is already being dreamed.
Without support, the dream will fade away
without effects.
For it is your support that strengthens it.

Healing might thus be called a counter-dream,
which cancels out the dream of sickness
in the name of truth.

The mind which understands that sickness
can be nothing but a dream
is not deceived by forms the dream may take.
Sickness where guilt is absent cannot come,
for it is but another form of guilt.
Atonement does not heal the sick,
for that is not a cure.
It takes away the guilt
that makes the sickness possible.
And that is cure indeed.

"Cure" is a word that cannot be applied
to any remedy the world accepts as beneficial.
What the world perceives as therapeutic
is but what will make the body "better."
When it tries to heal the mind,
it sees no separation from the body,
where it thinks the mind exists.
Its forms of healing thus must substitute
illusion for illusion.
One belief in sickness takes another form,
and so the patient now perceives himself as well.

He is not healed.
He merely had a dream that he was sick,
and in the dream he found a magic formula
to make him well.
Yet he has not awakened from the dream,
and so his mind remains exactly as it was before.
He has not seen the light
that would awaken him and end the dream.
What difference does the content
of a dream make in reality?
One either sleeps or wakens.
There is nothing in between.

You must learn the cost of sleeping,
and refuse to pay it.
Only then will you decide to awaken.

Healing is release from the fear of waking
and the substitution of the decision to wake.

Healing is freedom.
For it demonstrates that dreams
will not prevail against the truth.

Who would put his faith in dreams
once they are recognized for what they are?
Awareness of dreaming
is the real function of God's teachers.
They watch the dream figures come and go,
shift and change, suffer and die.
Yet they are not deceived by what they see.
They recognize that to behold a dream figure
as sick and separate is no more real
than to regard it as healthy and beautiful.
Unity alone is not a thing of dreams.
And it is this God's teachers acknowledge
as behind the dream, beyond all seeming
and yet surely theirs.

Looking Within

Healing does not come
from anyone else.
You must accept guidance
from within.

No one who comes here
but must still have hope,
some lingering illusion,
or some dream that there is something
outside of himself
that will bring happiness and peace to him.
If everything is in him
this cannot be so.

Seek not outside yourself.
For all your pain
comes simply from a futile search
for what you want,
insisting where it must be found.
What if it is not there?
Do you prefer that you be right or happy?
Be you glad that you are told
where happiness abides,
and seek no longer elsewhere.
You will fail.
But it is given you to know the truth,
and not to seek for it outside yourself.

Heal and be healed.
There is no other choice of pathways
that can ever lead to peace.

There is a sense of peace so deep
that no dream in this world
has ever brought even a dim imagining
of what it is.

Peace be to you to whom is healing offered.
And you will learn that peace is given you
when you accept the healing for yourself.
What occurred within the instant
that love entered in without attack
will stay forever.
Your healing will be one of its effects.

Brother, the war against yourself is almost over.
The journey's end is at the place of peace.
Would you not now accept
the peace offered you here?

Health is inner peace.

To have peace, teach peace.

Limit the peace you share,
and your Self must be unknown to you.

The purpose of your learning
is to enable you
to bring the quiet with you,
and to heal distress and turmoil.
This is not done by avoiding them
and seeking a haven of isolation
for yourself.

We who are one
would recognize this day
the truth about ourselves.
We would come home, and rest in unity.
For there is peace, and nowhere else
can peace be sought and found.

When peace comes at last
to those who wrestle with temptation
and fight against the giving in to sin;
when the light comes at last into the mind
given to contemplation;
or when the goal is finally achieved by anyone,
it always comes with just one happy realization;
"I need do nothing."

Psychotherapy

Psychotherapy is the only form of therapy there is.
Since only the mind can be sick,
only the mind can be healed.
Only the mind is in need of healing.
This does not appear to be the case,
for the manifestations of this world
seem real indeed.
Psychotherapy is necessary so that an individual
can begin to question their reality.
Sometimes he is able to start
to open his mind without formal help,
but even then it is always some change
in his perception of interpersonal relationships
that enables him to do so.
Sometimes he needs a more structured,
extended relationship with an "official" therapist.
Either way, the task is the same;
the patient must be helped to change his mind
about the "reality" of illusions.

Very simply, the purpose of psychotherapy
is to remove the blocks to truth.

Illness of any kind may be defined
as the result of a view of the self
as weak, vulnerable, evil and endangered,
and thus in need of constant defense.

Psychotherapy is a process
that changes the view of the self.

Psychotherapy, correctly understood,
teaches forgiveness and helps the patient
to recognize and accept it.

A therapist does not heal;
he lets healing be.

Who, then, is the therapist,
and who is the patient?
In the end everyone is both.
He who needs healing must heal.

Everyone is both patient and therapist
in every relationship in which he enters.

Forgiveness and Gratitude

To forgive is to heal.

Forgiveness removes only the untrue,
lifting the shadows from the world
and carrying it, safe and sure
within its gentleness.

Forgive all thoughts
which would oppose the truth
of your completion, unity and peace.

What is forgiveness
but a willingness that truth be true?
What can remain unhealed
and broken from a Unity
which holds all things within itself?

All that stood between your image of yourself
and what you are,
forgiveness washes joyfully away.

Pardon is always justified.
It has a sure foundation.

Forgiveness recognized as merited
will heal.

Do not forget today
that there can be no form of suffering
that fails to hide an unforgiving thought.
Nor can there be a form of pain
forgiveness cannot heal.

True forgiveness . . .
must heal the mind that gives,
for giving is receiving.

Rejoice in the power of forgiveness
to heal your sight completely.

Without the darkness of the past upon your eyes,
you cannot fail to see today.
And what you see will be so welcome
that you will gladly extend today forever.

In complete forgiveness,
in which you recognize
that there is nothing to forgive,
you are absolved completely.

Be glad indeed salvation asks so little,
not so much.
It asks for nothing in reality.
And even in illusions it but asks
forgiveness be the substitute for fear.

Those who have been forgiven
must devote themselves first to healing
because having received the idea of healing,
they must give it to hold it.

You understand that you are healed
when you give healing.
You accept forgiveness
as accomplished in yourself
when you forgive.
You recognize your brother as yourself,
and thus do you perceive
that you are whole.

Forgiveness is a choice.
I never see my brother as he is,
for that is far beyond perception.
What I see in him
is merely what I wish to see
because it stands for what
I want to be the truth.
It is to this alone that I respond,
however much I seem to be
impelled by outside happenings.

Look on your brother with the willingness
to see him as he is.
And do not keep a part of him
outside your willingness that he be healed.
To heal is to make whole.
And what is whole can have no missing parts
that have been kept outside.
Forgiveness rests on recognizing this.

In your forgiveness of this stranger,
alien to you and yet your ancient Friend,
lies his release and your redemption with him.

Think not that your forgiveness of your brother
serves but you two alone.
For the whole new world rests in the hands
of every two who enter here to rest.

Today we learn to think of gratitude
in place of anger, malice and revenge.
We have been given everything.
If we refuse to recognize it,
we are not entitled therefore to our bitterness,
and to a self-perception which regards
us in a place of merciless pursuit,
where we are badgered ceaselessly,
and pushed about without a thought or care
for us or for our future.
Gratitude becomes the single thought
we substitute for these insane perceptions.

Walk, then, in gratitude
the way of love.
For hatred is forgotten
when we lay comparisons aside.
What more remains
as obstacles to peace?

Then let our brothers
lean their tired heads
against our shoulders
as they rest awhile.
We offer thanks for them.
For if we can direct them
to the peace that we would find,
the way is opening at last to us.

When your forgiveness is complete
you will have total gratitude.

Forgiveness is the means
by which I will recognize my innocence.

My forgiveness is the means
by which the world is healed,
together with myself.
Let me, then, forgive the world,
that it may be healed along with me.

Reality and Truth

Reality is here.
It belongs to you and me and God,
and is perfectly satisfying to all of us.
Only this awareness heals,
because it is the awareness of truth.

Reality can dawn only on an unclouded mind.
It is always there to be accepted,
but its acceptance depends
on your willingness to have it.

What can be fearful but fantasy,
and who turns to fantasy unless he despairs
of finding satisfaction in reality?

You need reality to dispel your fears.
Would you not exchange your fears for truth,
if the exchange is yours for the asking?

Appearances deceive, but can be changed.
Reality is changeless. It does not deceive at all,
and if you fail to see beyond appearances
you are deceived.

We go beyond appearances today
and reach the source of healing.

Remember that you always choose
between truth and illusion.

So healing must replace
the fantasies of sickness.

Truth cannot fail to heal and heal forever.

Do not defend yourself
against the truth.

Let truth be what it is.
Do not intrude upon it,
do not attack it,
do not interrupt its coming.
Let it encompass every situation
and bring you peace.
Not even faith is asked of you,
for truth asks nothing.
Let it enter,
and it will call forth and secure for you
the faith you need for peace.

When truth has come
it harbors in its wings
the gift of perfect constancy,
and love which does not falter
in the face of pain.

When truth has come all pain is over,
for there is no room for transitory thoughts
and dead ideas to linger in your mind.
Truth occupies your mind completely,
liberating you from all beliefs in the ephemeral.
They have no place because the truth has come,
and they are nowhere.
They cannot be found,
for truth is everywhere forever, now.

Healing will flash across your open mind,
as peace and truth arise
to take the place of war
and vain imaginings.

To be healed is merely to accept
what has always been the simple truth,
and always will remain
exactly as it has forever been.

To believe in truth
you do not have to do anything.

We are concerned only
with giving welcome to the truth.

Truth merely wants to give you happiness,
for such its purpose is.

The truth of what we are
is not for words to speak of nor describe.
Yet we can realize our function here,
and words can speak of this and teach it, too,
if we exemplify the words in us.

Do not be confused about what must be healed,
but tell yourself:

   "I have forgotten what I really am.
   For I mistook my body for myself."

Ask the truth to come to us
and set us free.
And truth will come,
for it has never been apart from us.
It merely waits for just this invitation
which we give today.
We introduce it with a healing prayer,
to help us rise above defensiveness,
and let truth be as it has always been:

   "Sickness is a defense against the truth.
   I will accept the truth of what I am,
   And let my mind be wholly healed today."

5

THE JOY OF FREEDOM

The end of dreaming brings an end to fear and pain. With awakening, says the *Course*, comes the love, peace, and joy of freedom. Even before complete awakening, we receive glimpses of this state. These glimpses come through what *A Course in Miracles* calls *vision* and *a holy instant*. A holy instant is one in which we directly experience our true nature and reality. Vision is the inner seeing that pictures this reality to us. The *Course* emphasizes that the holy instant and vision have enormous healing power, both for ourselves and for others, because reality itself is healing. But reality offers more than healing: in it we are filled with love, peace, and joy beyond our wildest dreams. For ultimately we are beyond all dreams, and the end of dreaming is a gift of healing.

> *To love yourself*
> *is to heal yourself.*

The Holy Instant

The holy instant
is this instant
and every instant.

The holy instant is eternal,
and your illusions of time
will not prevent the timeless
from being what it is,
nor you from experiencing it as it is.

What is the holy instant
but God's appeal to you
to recognize what He has given you?
Here is the great appeal to reason;
the awareness of what is always there to see,
the happiness that could be always yours.
Here is the constant peace
you could experience forever.

The instant of holiness is shared,
and cannot be yours alone.
Remember, then, when you are tempted
to attack a brother,
that his instant of release is yours.
Miracles are the instants of release you offer,
and will receive.

Forget not that your relationship is one,
and so it must be
that whatever threatens the peace of one
is an equal threat to the other.
The power of joining its blessing lies in the fact
that it is now impossible for you or your brother
to experience fear alone,
or to attempt to deal with it alone.

Never believe that this is necessary,
or even possible.
Yet just as this is impossible,
so is it equally impossible
that the holy instant come to either of you
without the other.
And it will come to both
at the request of either.

Whoever is saner at the time
[a] threat is perceived should remember
how deep is his indebtedness to the other
and how much gratitude is due him,
and be glad that he can pay his debt
by bringing happiness to both.
Let him remember this, and say:

> "I desire this holy instant for myself,
> that I may share it with my brother,
> whom I love.
> It is not possible
> that I can have it without him,
> or he without me.
> Yet it is wholly possible
> for us to share it now.
> And so I choose this instant
> as the one to offer to the Holy Spirit,
> that His blessing may descend on us,
> and keep us both in peace."

And may the holy instant
speed you on the way,
as it will surely do
if you but let it come to you.

Vision and Wholeness

Vision will correct the perception
of everything you see.

Everything looked upon with vision
is healed and holy.

Recognizing that what I see
reflects what I think I am,
I realize that vision is my greatest need.
The world I see attests to the fearful nature
of the self-image I have made.
If I would remember who I am,
it is essential
that I let this image of myself go.
As it is replaced by truth,
vision will surely be given me.
And with this vision,
I will look upon the world
and on myself
with charity and love.

Vision will come to you
at first in glimpses,
but they will be enough
to show you what is given you
who see your brother sinless.

Forget not that the choice
of sin or truth, helplessness or power,
is the choice of whether to attack or heal.
For healing comes of power
and attack of helplessness.
Whom you attack you cannot want to heal.
And whom you would have healed
must be the one you chose
to be protected from attack.

And what is this decision but the choice
whether to see him through the body's eyes,
or let him be revealed to you through vision?
How this decision leads to its effects
is not your problem.
But what you want to see
must be your choice.

To your tired eyes I bring a vision
of a different world,
so new and clean and fresh
you will forget the pain and sorrow
that you saw before.
Yet this a vision is
which you must share
with everyone you see,
for otherwise you will behold it not.
To give this gift is how to make it yours.

Vision, being healed, has power to heal.
This is the light that brings
your peace of mind to other minds,
to share it and be glad
that they are one with you
and with themselves.
This is the light that heals.

Everything looked upon with vision
falls gently into place.

Vision sets all things right,
bringing them gently
within the kindly sway
of Heaven's laws.

Vision is the means by which the Holy Spirit
translates your nightmares into happy dreams;
your wild hallucinations that show you
all the fearful outcomes of imagined sin
into the calm and reassuring sights
with which He would replace them.
These gentle sights and sounds
are looked on happily, and heard with joy.

Hallucinations disappear
when they are recognized for what they are.
This is the healing and the remedy.
Believe them not and they are gone.
And all you need to do is recognize
that you did this.
Once you accept this simple fact
and take into yourself the power you gave them,
you are released from them.

You have the vision now
to look past all illusions.

Your vision has become the greatest power
for the undoing of illusion
that God Himself could give.

Let us lift up our eyes together,
not in fear but faith.
And there will be no fear in us,
for in our vision will be no illusions;
only a pathway to the open door of Heaven,
the home we share in quietness
and where we live in gentleness and peace,
as one together.

There is no problem, no event or situation,
no perplexity that vision will not solve.
All is redeemed when looked upon with vision.

Christ's vision has one law.
It does not look upon a body,
and mistake it for the Son whom God created.
It beholds a light beyond the body;
an idea beyond what can be touched,
a purity undimmed by errors, pitiful mistakes,
and fearful thoughts of guilt from dreams of sin.
It sees no separation.
And it looks on everyone,
on every circumstance, all happenings
and all events,
without the slightest fading
of the light it sees.

This can be taught; and must be taught
by all who would achieve it.
It requires but the recognition
that the world cannot give anything
that faintly can compare with this in value;
nor set up a goal that does not merely disappear
when this has been perceived.

What is a miracle but this remembering?

Child of peace, the light has come to you.
The light you bring you do not recognize,
and yet you will remember.
Who can deny himself the vision
that he brings to others?

Healing is a sign
that you want to make whole.

Those whom you heal
bear witness to your healing,
for in their wholeness
you will see your own.

Sanity is wholeness,
and the sanity of your brothers
is yours.

To be wholehearted you must be happy.
If fear and love cannot coexist,
and if it is impossible to be wholly fearful
and remain alive,
the only possible whole state
is the wholly joyous.
To heal or to make joyous
is therefore the same as to integrate
and to make one.

Our minds are whole
because they are one.

By healing you learn of wholeness,
and by learning of wholeness
you learn to remember God.

Completion lies first in union,
and then in the extension of union.

Christ waits for your acceptance
of Him as yourself,
and of His Wholeness
as yours.

The wholeness of God,
which is His peace,
cannot be appreciated
except by a whole mind
that recognizes the wholeness
of God's creation.

Beyond the body, beyond the sun and stars,
past everything you see and yet somehow familiar,
is an arc of golden light
that stretches as you look
into a great and shining circle.
And all the circle fills with light
before your eyes.
The edges of the circle disappear,
and what is in it is no longer contained at all.
The light expands and covers everything,
extending to infinity forever shining
and with no break or limit anywhere.
Within it everything is joined
in perfect continuity.
Nor is it possible to imagine
that anything could be outside,
for there is nowhere
that this light is not.

Here is the meaning of what you are;
a part of this with all of it within,
and joined to all as all is joined in you.
Accept the vision that can show you this.

The Atonement is not the price
of your wholeness,
but it is the price
of your awareness of your wholeness.

The Atonement is but the way back
to what was never lost.

The purpose of Atonement
is to dispel illusions,
not to establish them as real
and then forgive them.

Accept Atonement and you are healed.

Between the future and the past
the laws of God must intervene,
if you would free yourself.
Atonement stands between them
like a lamp shining so brightly
that the chain of darkness
in which you bound yourself
will disappear.

You do not know your joy
because you do not know
your own Self-fullness.
Exclude any part of the Kingdom from yourself
and you are not whole.
A split mind cannot perceive its fullness,
and needs the miracle of its wholeness
to dawn upon it and heal it.
This reawakens the wholeness in it.

Your Self-fullness is as boundless as God's.
Like His, It extends forever
and in perfect peace.
Its radiance is so intense
that It creates in perfect joy,
and only the whole
can be born of Its wholeness.

Love and Joy

Lay forgiveness on your mind
and let all fear be gently laid aside,
that love may find its rightful place in you.

Perceive in sickness
but another call for love,
and offer your brother
what he believes
he cannot offer himself.

If you would look upon love,
which is the world's reality,
how could you do better than to recognize,
in every defense against it,
the underlying appeal for it?
And how could you better learn of its reality
than by answering the appeal for it
by giving it?

Understanding brings appreciation
and appreciation brings love.

Exempt no one from your love,
or you will be hiding a dark place in your mind
where the Holy Spirit is not welcome.
And thus you will exempt yourself
from His healing power,
for by not offering total love
you will not be healed completely.

When you want only love
you will see nothing else.

What occurred within the instant
that love entered in without attack
will stay forever.
Your healing will be one of its effects.

You will identify
with what you think will make you safe.
Whatever it may be,
you will believe that it is one with you.
Your safety lies in truth, and not in lies.
Love is your safety.
Fear does not exist.
Identify with love, and you are safe.
Identify with love, and you are home.
Identify with love, and find your Self.

Love is your power.

Brother we heal together
as we live together
and love together.

Healing is a thought
by which two minds
perceive their oneness
and become glad.

You are sad
because you are not fulfilling your function
as co-creator with God,
and are therefore depriving yourself of joy.

To heal is to make happy.
I have told you to think
how many opportunities you have had
to gladden yourself,
and how many you have refused.
This is the same as telling you
that you have refused to heal yourself.

Think of this awhile:
The world you see does nothing.
It has no effects at all.
It merely represents your thoughts.
And it will change entirely
as you elect to change your mind,
and choose the joy of God
as what you really want.
Your Self is radiant in this holy joy,
unchanged, unchanging and unchangeable,
forever and forever.

The light that belongs to you
is the light of joy.
Radiance is not associated with sorrow.
Joy calls forth
an integrated willingness to share it,
and promotes the mind's natural impulse
to respond as one.
Those who attempt to heal
without being wholly joyous themselves
call forth different kinds of responses
at the same time,
and thus deprive others
of the joy of responding wholeheartedly.

Joy is unified purpose.

Joy and peace are not but idle dreams.
They are your right,
because of what you are.

Truth replaces fear,
and joy becomes what you expect
to take the place of pain.

Will you not answer
the call of love with joy?

Only the healed mind
can experience revelation
with lasting effect,
because revelation is an experience
of pure joy.

Only joy increases forever,
since joy and eternity are inseparable.

We are free to choose our joy instead of pain,
our holiness in place of sin,
the peace of God instead of conflict,
and the light of Heaven
for the darkness of the world.

The Light in You

There is a light that this world cannot give.
Yet you can give it, as it was given you.
And as you give it, it shines forth
to call you from the world and follow it.
For this light will attract you
as nothing in this world can do.

Ask for light
and learn that you are light.

Sit quietly and close your eyes.
The light within you is sufficient.
It alone has power
to give the gift of sight to you.
Exclude the outer world,
and let your thoughts fly
to the peace within.
They know the way.

In shining peace within you
is the perfect purity
in which you were created.
Fear not to look upon the lovely truth in you.
Look past darkness to the holy place
where you will see the light.

Shining purity,
wholly untouched by guilt
and wholly loving,
is bright within you.

Light is unlimited,
and spreads across this world
in quiet joy.

Only you can deprive yourself of anything.
Do not oppose this realization,
for it is truly the beginning
of the dawn of light.
Remember also that the denial
of this simple fact takes many forms,
and these you must learn to recognize
and to oppose steadfastly, without exception.
This is a crucial step in the reawakening.

The past can cast no shadow
to darken the present,
unless you are afraid of the light.
And only if you are would you choose
to bring darkness with you,
and by holding it in your mind,
see it as a dark cloud
that shrouds your brothers
and conceals their reality from your sight.

Dreams disappear
when light has come
and you can see.

Alone we are all lowly,
but together we shine
with brightness so intense
that none of us alone
can even think of it.

Each one you see in light
brings your light closer to your awareness.

Behold your brothers in their freedom,
and learn from them how to be free of darkness.
The light in you will waken them,
and they will not leave you asleep.

The lamp is lit in both of you for one another.
And by the hands that gave it to your brother
shall both of you be led past fear to love.

Every chance given him to heal
is another opportunity
to replace darkness with light
and fear with love.
If he refuses it he binds himself to darkness,
because he did not choose to free his brother
and enter light with him.

All those you brought with you
will shine on you,
and you will shine on them in gratitude
because they brought you here.
Your light will join with theirs
in power so compelling,
that it will draw the others out of darkness
as you look on them.

The light in one awakens it in all.
And when you see it in your brother,
you are remembering for everyone.

The light that joins you
shines throughout the universe,
and because it joins you,
so it makes you one with your Creator.

Rest in God

When you heal,
you are remembering the laws of God
and forgetting the laws of the ego.

Healing, then,
is a way of approaching knowledge
by thinking in accordance
with the laws of God,
and recognizing their universality.

Where two have joined for healing,
God is there.

Everyone is equally entitled to His gift
of healing and deliverance and peace.

No one can lose and everyone must gain
whenever any gift of God
has been requested and received by anyone.

Be not restless,
for you undertake a quiet journey
to the peace of God.

"I rest in God."
Completely undismayed,
this thought will carry you
through storms and strife
past misery and pain, past loss and death,
and onward to the certainty of God.
There is no suffering it cannot heal.
There is no problem that it cannot solve.
And no appearance but will turn to truth
before the eyes of you who rest in God.

This is the day of peace.
You rest in God,
and while the world is torn by winds of hate
your rest remains completely undisturbed.
Yours is the rest of truth.

As you close your eyes,
sink into stillness.
Let these periods of rest and respite
reassure your mind
that all its frantic fantasies
were but the dreams of fever
that has passed away.
Let it be still
and thankfully accept its healing.
No more fearful dreams will come,
now that you rest in God.

References

To facilitate further study, we have referenced each passage included in this book, citing the volume and page number from which it was excerpted. WB stands for *Workbook*, T for *Text*, MT for *Manual for Teachers*, and P for *Psychotherapy*. The page numbers refer to the first edition of the *Course*. *A Course in Miracles* may be ordered from bookstores or from the Foundation for Inner Peace, P.O. Box 598, Mill Valley, CA 94942. Cassette-tape readings of the three parts of this book—*Accept This Gift*, *A Gift of Peace*, and *A Gift of Healing*—are available from Audio Renaissance Tapes, 6 Commerce Way, Arden, NC 28704, (800) 452–5589.

Accept This Gift

THE PATH OF LIGHT

WB 347. *The Nature of the* Course: WB 321; T 132; T 13; T464; T Intro; WB 103. *Miracles:* T 1; T 203; T 1; T549; T 390; WB 466. *Purpose:* T 341; MT 22; T 100; T 405; WB 341; WB 380. *Choice:* T 418; T 164; T 620; T 332; WB 352; T 418. *Truth and Reality:* T 139; T 74; T 152; T 234; T 412; T 429; T 267; T 150; T 271; T 149; T Intro; T 371; WB 410.

THE MIND

T 131. *Mind:* WB 297; T 77; WB 238; T 9; T 359; T 360; T 113; WB 339; WB 312; WB 372; WB 400. *Belief:* T 124; T 116; T 464; WB 15; WB 189. *Thought:* WB 26; WB 34; WB 119; T 114; T 25; WB 461. *Perception:* T 35; T 7; T 192; T 73; T 425; T 196; WB 349; WB 45; T 301; MT 48; WB 441.

DREAMS AND ILLUSIONS

T 351. *Dreams:* T 351; T 351; T 473; T 552. T 351; T 579; WB 143; WB 340; WB 339; T 554; WB 410. *Illusions:* T 316; T 439; T 143; T 598; T 439; T 453; T 121; WB 189; WB 346; MT 35; WB 95; WB 83.

THE WORLD AND TIME

T 73. *The World:* T 415; T 545; WB 233; WB 226; WB 236; WB 361; T 476; WB 48. *Time:* T 168; T 230; T 234; T 233; T 234; T 234; T 281; WB 233; WB 236; WB 304; WB 329; WB 432.

MISTAKEN IDENTITY

T 51. *Body:* WB 372; T 504; WB 372; T 389; T 619; WB 415; T 143; T 560; T 142; WB 355; T 301; MT 55; WB 378. *Ego:* T 77; T 121; T 364; T 121; T 61; T 128; T 144; WB 114; T 274; T 137; T 290; WB

187. *Self-Concept*: WB 155; WB 246; T 118; WB 227; T 617; T 612; WB 252.

TRUE IDENTITY

WB 431. *Identity*: WB 260; T 285; WB 445; WB 354; WB 415; WB 473; WB 449. *Self*: T 168; T 574; T 358; WB 63; T 490; T 49; WB 159; WB 195; WB 219. *Spirit*: T 7; WB 167; T 9.

OBSTACLES ON THE PATH

WB 73. *Pain*: WB 351; WB 351; T 402; WB 179; T 430; T 573; WB 354; WB 352; WB 351; WB 429. *Guilt*: T 221; T 57; T 77; T 223; T 246; T 247; T 515; T 78; T 258; WB 370. *Fear*: WB 402; WB 77; T 198; T 26; T 28; T 202; T 202; T 202; T 204; T 267; T 558; T 92; WB 418. *Anger and Attack*: T 200; T 487; T 297; T 119; T 37; T 451; T 92; WB 40; T 593. *Judgment*: T 42; T 42; T 44; T 237; T 411; T 466; T 606; WB 446; MT 27; WB 83. *Defensiveness*: T 446; MT 13; WB 245; WB 245; MT 12; WB 248; WB 248; MT 39; WB 277.

HEALING RELATIONSHIPS

T 147. *Practicing Forgiveness*: T 260; MT 50; WB 213; T 11; T 298; T 329; T 513; T 393; T 393; T 509; T 516; T 518; T 568; WB 213; T 504; WB 103; WB 73; WB 391: WB 210; WB 464. *Teaching and Learning*: T 605; T 416; T 449; T 84; MT 1; MT 1; T 48 T 86; T 92; T 92; WB 278; MT 1; T 118; T 92; T 92. *Recognizing Your Brother*: T 132; T 193; T 201; T 108; T 242; T 405; T 446; T 491; T 543; T 568; T 156; T 163; WB 474. *Healing and Wholeness*: T 371; T 19; T 240; T 127; T 198; T 203; T 271; T 354; T 535; T 553; WB 255; MT 53; WB 252; T 24. *The Holy Relationship*: T 424; T 435; T 119; T 8; T 132; T 317; T 346; T 448; T 353; T 136; WB 166.

THE PEACEFUL ALTERNATIVE

T 455. *Coming Home*: T 316; T 139; T 240; T 222; T 354; WB 331. *Freedom*: T 30; WB 356; T 174; T 13; WB 373; T 306. *Salvation*: T 616; T 590; T 614; T 613; T 445; WB 168. *Love*: T 55; T 315; T 238; T 215; T 217; T 382; T 292; T 366; WB 315; WB 363; MT 21; WB 318; WB 225; WB 226; T 120; WB 396. *Awakening to God*: T 218; WB 413; T 136; T 574; WB 177; T 139; WB 322. *The Conditions of Peace*: MT 28; T 15; WB 340; WB 339; WB 339; T 92; T 134; T 216; WB 194; T 341; T 452; T 363; T 461; T 490; WB 340; WB 347; WB 348. *Light and Joy*: WB 102; T 352; WB 347; T 66; T 592; WB 305; WB 103; WB 186.

A NEW BEGINNING

T 613; T 602; WB 221; WB 350.

A Gift of Peace

THE CHOICE IS OURS

T 412. *Deciding for Peace*: WB 220; T 134; T 78; T 255; T 541; T

285; T 285; T 118; T 418; T 56; T 489; WB 320; T 489; WB 274. *Our Shared Purpose*: T 61; T 472; T 463; T 71; T 448–449; T 581; WB 261; WB 413.

CHANGING YOUR MIND ABOUT YOUR MIND

WB 51. *The Power of Mind*: T 134; T 113; T 26; T 397; WB 236; WB 31; WB 78; WB 78; WB 76; T 9; WB 167; MT 49; WB 238; WB 339–340; T 136; WB 392. *Perception Is a Mirror*: T 7; T 168; T 192; T 200; T 425; T 613; T 425; T 483; T 607; T 35; WB 403; WB 94. *The Power of Thought*: WB 26; WB 26; WB 454; T 98; T 5; WB 87; WB 26.

CHANGING WHAT YOU THINK IS REAL

T 149. *Dreaming*: T 574; T 574; T 238; T 169; T 571–572; WB 427; T 569; T 568; WB 193. *The Cost of Illusions*: T 320; T 118; T 231; T 229; T 461; T 315; T 385; T 315; WB 128; T 325; T 446–447; T 562; MT 87; WB 189. *Letting Go of the Past*: T 240; T 574; T 234; T 234; T 324; T 324; WB 130; T 325; T 292; T 282; T 281; T 234–235; T 281–282; WB 195; T 604; T 280; T 386; MT 58. *Welcoming Reality*: T 184; T 146; T 152; T 198; T 445; WB 419.

THE OBSTACLES TO PEACE

T 392. *The Pursuit of Specialness*: T 467; T 467; T 466; T 473; T 467; T 470. *The Meaning of Sacrifice*: MT 32; T 302; T 302; T 304–305; T 564; T 306. *The Veil of Fear and Guilt*: T 380; T 276; WB 21; WB 231; T 596; T 240; T 446; T 264; T 399; WB 403; WB 365; WB 458; T 382; T 344; T 244; T 220; T 245; T 221; T 246; T 292; T 289; T 305; WB 114; T 244; T 255; T 247; WB 428. *Releasing Judgment and Defense*: T 43; T 42; T 156; WB 389; WB 470; T 411; MT 37; T 461; WB 277; T 17; WB 252; WB 318; T 204; WB 332; WB 248.

THE END OF CONFLICT

WB 459. *Reinterpreting Anger and Attack*: MT 42; MT 44; T 569; T 120; T 202; T 200; T 37; WB 40; T 89; T 88; T 128; T 92; T 209; T 488; MT 12; T 92; WB 297; WB 147; WB 89. *The Resolution of Conflict and War*: WB 458; T 475; MT 11; T 455; MT 10; T 533; T 454; T 312; T 454; T 83.

PEACE TO MY BROTHER, WHO IS ONE WITH ME

WB 292. *The Errors of Ego*: MT 77; T 53; MT 77; T 155; T 128; T 73; MT 79; T 57. *You Are One Self*: WB 166; T 92; T 246; WB 175; T 46; WB 118; WB 80; T 186; WB 261; WB 410. *Knowing Your Brother*: T 61; T 444; T 132; T 513; T 137; T 76; T 132; T 72; T 405; T 492; T 440; T 63; T 203; T 62; T 449; T 570; T 242; T 571; T 604; T 616; T 621; T 8; WB 469; T 304; T 518; T 139; WB 115; WB 474.

IT IS THROUGH US THAT PEACE WILL COME

WB 220. *To Teach Is to Learn*: T 92; MT 5; T 98–99; T 128; T 608; T 96; T 74. *To Give Is to Receive*: T 617; T 397; T 293; T 490; WB 192;

T 24. *To Let Forgiveness Rest upon All Things*; T 473; T 370; T 329; T 330; T 325; T 460; T 393; T 461; T 394; T 516; T 528; T 568; T 572; T 594; T 593; WB 458; WB 210; WB 391; WB 391; WB 370; WB 408; WB 73; WB 244; WB 83. *To Bring Peace to the World*: T 488; WB 310; T 540; T 585; T 585; MT 35; WB 348; WB 349; WB 349; T 432; WB 361; WB 145.

THE GIFTS OF PEACE

WB 293. *Healing*: T 434; T 182; WB 252; T 147; T 350; T 203; T 535; T 235; WB 264; WB 255–256; WB 419. *Freedom*: WB 356; WB 354; WB 48; WB 335; WB 458. *Love*: T 226; T 227; T 237; T Intro; T 12; T 82; T 293; T 274; T 219; T 321; T 408; T 407; T 407; T 267; WB 231; WB 445; T 260; T 522; MT 55; WB 444; WB 453; WB 115.

THE WAY TO PEACE IS OPEN

T 279. *The Way to Peace Is Open*: WB 304; T 44; T 278; T 33; WB 352; T 446; T 74; T 518; T 39; T 184; T 177; T 238; WB 339; WB 340; WB 374.

A Gift of Healing

THE DESIRE FOR HEALING

T 228. *The Decision to Heal*: T 182; T 215; T 489; T 598; T 214; MT 19; T 350; WB 316. *The Conditions of Healing*: T 553; T 201; T 201; T 160; T 111; T 529; T 535; T 134; T 180; T 535; T 535; T 535; WB 255. *Healing One Another*: T 134; WB 254; WB 261; T 490; WB 255; T 529; T 529; T 530; T 430; WB 364; T 155; T 529; T 366; T 378; T 245; WB 475; T 399.

THE DREAM OF SICKNESS

WB 73. *The Veil of Illusion*: T 188; T 318; T 408; T 591; T 588; MT 23; T 323; T 559. *Separation Is Sickness*: T 207; T 241; WB 421; T 202; MT 54; T 148; MT 17; MT 16; T 182; T 172; T 172; WB 265. *Limitations of the Body*: T 97; T 560; T 140; T 560; T 177; WB 372; T 97; T 140; T 140; T 142; T 143; T 143; T 141; T 146; T 142; T 97; T 301; WB 378. *The World You See*: T 251; T 19; T 539; T 537; T 536; T 212; T 539; T 591; T 536; WB 256; WB 420. *Time and Eternity*: T 240; T 156; T 230; WB 11; T 513; WB 13; T 240; T 324; T 241; T 79; T 178; T 272; T 322; T 282; T 283; T 520; T 235; WB 443; T 519; WB 360; WB 361; WB 360. *From Fear to Faith*: T 110; T 202; P 9; T 152; T 198; T 267; T 172; T 112; T 152; T 112; T 394; T 373; T 374; T 373; WB 435.

THE CAUSES OF THE DREAM

T 543. *Attack and Blame*: T 200; P 19; WB 475; T 272; T 187; T 187; T 187. *Escape from Guilt*: P 10; T 255; T 256; T 217; T 245; T 245; T 263; T 385; T 264; T 263; T 283; T 258. *The Power of Perception*: T 430; T 428; T 214; T 341; WB 329; T 332; T 429; T 123; T 106; T

148; WB 365; WB 454; WB 428; WB 348; WB 429. *Learning and Teaching*: T 275; T 278; T 620; T 183; T 251; T 183; WB 357; WB 325; T 103; T 75; MT 54; MT 45; T 87. *A Change of Mind*: WB 236; P 8; MT 17; T 174; T 148; T 148; T 549; T 175; T 113; T 127; WB 456.

THE MEANS OF AWAKENING

T 147. *Awakening from the Dream*: T 551; T 327; T 551; T 551; WB 263; WB 263; T 551; T 553; T 553; WB 254; WB 263; WB 263; T 213; T 147; WB 255; MT 31. *Looking Within*: T 134; T 573; T 573; P 16; T 249; T 537; T 453; T 15; T 100; T 186; WB 80; WB 416; T 363. *Psychotherapy*: P 1; P 1; P 9; P 3; P 1; T 161; P 13; P 18. *Forgiveness and Gratitude*: MT 53; T 370; WB 175; T 516; T 592; T 593; T 594; WB 370; WB 223; WB 131; WB 131; T 298; T 590; T 76; WB 293; WB 460; T 595; T 396; T 404; WB 363; WB 363; WB 363; WB 363; WB 99; WB 145. *Reality and Truth*: T 159; T 174; T 158; T 199; T 597; WB 264; T 325; WB 255; WB 264; T 196; T 345; WB 189; WB 189; WB 252; WB 254; T 200; WB 469; WB 252; WB 469; WB 253; WB 252.

THE JOY OF FREEDOM

T 198. *The Holy Instant*: T 288; T 325; T 434; T 282; T 358; T 358; T 323. *Vision and Wholeness*: T 218; T 415; WB 91; T 411; T 432; T 621; WB 191; T 413; T 413; T 414; T 413; T 398; T 398; T 398; T 413; WB 292; T 417; T 448; WB 88; T 183; T 235; T 82; T 66; T 147; T 110; T 318; T 187; T 88; T 417; T 417; T 209; T 219; T 246; MT 53; T 243; T 123; T 123. *Love and Joy*: T 198; WB 176; T 203; T 202; T 115; T 227; T 215; T 537; WB 415; T 115; T 198; T 66; T 117; T 66; WB 352; T 66; T 143; WB 183; WB 182; T 180; T 66; T 105; WB 352. *The Light in You*: T 235; T 131; WB 348; T 246; T 247; T 236; T 186; T 233; T 232; T 248; T 235; T 254; T 399; T 256; T 236; T 417; T 450. *Rest in God*: T 109; T 110; P 11; T 502; WB 341; T 240; WB 193; WB 193; WB 193.

Other Books by the Editors and Photographer

BY ROGER WALSH AND FRANCES VAUGHAN
Paths Beyond Ego: The Transpersonal Vision

BY FRANCES VAUGHAN
Awakening Intuition
The Inward Arc: Healing in Psychotherapy and Spirituality
Shadows of the Sacred

BY ROGER WALSH
The Spirit of Shamanism

BY JANE ENGLISH
Different Doorway: Adventures of a Caesarean-Born

ILLUSTRATED BY JANE ENGLISH
Tao Te Ching, by Lao Tsu
(with Gia-Fu Feng)
Chuang Tsu — Inner Chapters
(with Gia-Fu Feng)
Waterchild
(with Judith Bolinger)

About the Authors

Frances Vaughan, Ph.D., is a psychologist in private practice in Mill Valley, California, and author of *The Inward Arc* and *Awakening Intuition*. She is on the clinical faculty of the University of California Medical School at Irvine, and was formerly president of the Association for Transpersonal Psychology and the Association for Humanistic Psychology.

Roger Walsh, M.D., Ph.D., is professor of psychiatry, philosophy and anthropology at the University of California at Irvine. He has published more than one hundred scientific articles and fifteen books, and his writings have received over a dozen national and international awards.

Jane English's photographs have been published in translations of two of the Chinese Taoist classics, *Tao Te Ching* by Lao Tsu, and *Inner Chapters* by Chuang Tsu.